T0361782

ROUTLEDGE LIBRARY EDITIONS:
INTERNATIONAL BUSINESS

INTERNATIONAL
ENTREPRENEURSHIP

INTERNATIONAL ENTREPRENEURSHIP

The Effect of Firm Age on Motives for Internationalization

CANDIDA G. BRUSH

Volume 5

LONDON AND NEW YORK

First published in 1995

This edition first published in 2013
by Routledge
2 Park Square, Milton Park, Abingdon, Oxon, OX14 4RN

Simultaneously published in the USA and Canada
by Routledge
711 Third Avenue, New York, NY 10017

Routledge is an imprint of the Taylor & Francis Group, an informa business

British Library Cataloguing in Publication Data
A catalogue record for this book is available from the British Library

ISBN: 978-0-415-63009-2 (Set)
eISBN: 978-0-203-07716-0 (Set)
ISBN: 978-0-415-63953-8 (Volume 5)
eISBN: 978-0-203-07711-5 (Volume 5)

Publisher's Note
The publisher has gone to great lengths to ensure the quality of this reprint but
points out that some imperfections in the original copies may be apparent.

Disclaimer
The publisher has made every effort to trace copyright holders and would
welcome correspondence from those they have been unable to trace.

Printed and bound by CPI Group (UK) Ltd, Croydon, CR0 4YY

INTERNATIONAL ENTREPRENEURSHIP

The Effect of Firm Age on Motives for Internationalization

CANDIDA G. BRUSH

GARLAND PUBLISHING, Inc.
NEW YORK & LONDON / 1995

Library of Congress Cataloging-in-Publication Data

Brush, Candida G.
   International entrepreneurship : the effect of firm age on motives for
internationalization / Candida G. Brush.
      p.   cm. — (Garland studies in entrepreneurship)
   Includes bibliographical references and index.
   ISBN 0-8153-1978-9
   1. International business enterprises.   2. Entrepreneurship.
I. Title.   II. Series.
HD2755.5.B78   1995
338.8'8—dc20

94-43144
CIP

Printed on acid-free, 250-year-life paper
Manufactured in the United States of America

To David, Julie, Lucy and Emily who
inspired and supported me in this effort.

Contents

List of Tables and Exhibits

List of Appendices

Preface

My interest in the topic of international entrepreneurship was motivated in part by an investigation of women's enterprise creation in 24 OECD countries, and in part by a chance meeting with an international entrepreneur. In 1991, I was renting an office from a man who had created a biotechnology company and taken it public. He was starting a second business that manufactured medical equipment for testing cholesterol. One day, I asked him about his new venture and I learned that the business was less than one year old, had facilities in Boston and London, and was receiving revenues from product sales throughout Europe. In other words, my landlord had created an entrepreneurial endeavor that was also international. Excited by his story, I decided to investigate the international business activities of entrepreneurial firms. However, when I began my literature review, I found little in the field of Entrepreneurship that specifically addressed their international activities. Likewise when I explored the literature of International Business, I discovered no research about international activities of entrepreneurial companies.

This lack of research is not surprising. Studies in International Business have focused on firm investment, growth, and expansion activities of large multinational enterprises (MNE's), the segment of businesses most frequently engaging in international activities. Historically, success internationally was predicated on sufficient size, market power, and experience because political instability, geographic distance, and foreign economic policies often created high risks for firms investing or selling abroad.

Recently major environmental changes have occurred. Global political transitions such as the opening of new markets in the Czech Republics, Russia and Vietnam, rapid developments in telecommunications, implementation of the North American Free Trade Agreement (NAFTA) and U.S. export trade assistance programs have made it easier for companies that are young and innovative (entrepreneurial) to internationalize.

Since 1991 when this research was conducted, academic interest in the topic of "international entrepreneurship" also has grown and several recent articles have been published. Case studies by Patricia McDougall and Benjamin Oviatt (1993, 1994) found that contrary to existing theories and previous studies, some new companies are in fact "global" from the start, receiving resources and selling products in multiple countries.

My study, along with work by McDougall and Oviatt, provide important benchmarks for the integration of entrepreneurship and international business. This new stream of research differs from work in international business because it extends beyond the firm as a single unit of analysis, instead including the role of the founder/entrepreneur. In addition, this pushes the boundary of entrepreneurship research by extending the level of involvement beyond only domestic activities. Exploration of this new domain will not only suggest possibilities for theory revision or development but also provide information about an under-researched segment of companies.

My investigation of the intersection of two disciplines made this research task both exciting and daunting. I hope other researchers will continue the exploration of companies that are both international and entrepreneurial, further mapping out this domain.

Introduction

BACKGROUND

Rapid technological and telecommunications innovations have made it easier for small companies to internationalize. In addition, global political changes such as the opening of markets in Vietnam and the Czech Republics, the implementation of the North American Free Trade Agreements (NAFTA), and the successful conclusion of the General Agreement of Tariffs and Trade (GATT), create a favorable climate and new opportunities for small companies to internationalize[1]. These developments parallel U.S. policy on participation in international trade by small businesses[2]; "One important mission of the U.S. Small Business Administration is to encourage small and medium-sized firms to export their products to other nations (*Small Business in the American Economy*, 1988, p. iii). The U.S. Government is encouraging greater participation in international trade by small companies for three reasons; their survival, to improve the balance of trade, and to take advantage of growth opportunities in the world economy (*Small Business in the American Economy*, 1988, p. iii). Initiatives to improve access to international trade include the opening of export assistance centers in major cities such as Baltimore, Miami and Chicago (Maynard, 1994).

The Small Business Administration (SBA) recently estimated about 90,000 small firms exported to foreign markets, those with fewer than 100 employees accounting for nearly twenty-five percent of the total, or 22,000 enterprises (*Small Business in the American Economy*, 1988, p.6). While the U.S. Government does not collect statistics on international trade by size or age of enterprise, one segment of small companies increasingly involved in international markets are new ventures[3]. Anecdotal evidence of new small ventures exporting, licensing or investing abroad at start-up has recently appeared in the popular press. The Brooklyn Brewery (*Wall Street Journal*, Oct. 13, 1990) and Quantum Epitaxial Designs (*Nation's Business*, September, 1991), and Barnyard

Babies (Maynard, 1994) are three companies that exported at an early age.

New ventures are an important source of job creation (*Small Business in the American Economy*, 1988; Kirchoff and Phillips, 1988) and innovation (Birch, 1987). Each year more than 600,000 new small businesses are created (*Small Business in the American Economy*, 1988, p. 65, *The State of Small Business*, 1990, pp. 9-11), providing proportionately more jobs (Kirchoff & Phillips, 1988; *The State of Small Business*, 1989, pp. 13-16) and innovations than established companies. Despite their importance, new small companies and their early business activities are under-researched (Donckle, 1989). Furthermore, while scores of studies exist about the exporting activities of established small companies (Miesenbock, 1988) there are only a few studies that have considered internationalization by young small companies. Because of the liability of newness faced by new ventures (Stinchcombe, 1965) it might be argued that small companies internationalizing at an early age face greater risks than small companies internationalizing later in their life. Hence, a greater understanding of reasons for early or late internationalization, and resultant extent of activities abroad would appear to be of great interest.

In spite of this recent international activity by new companies, studies on this topic from the field of Entrepreneurship are limited. An emerging body of research has explored globalization of new ventures (Oviatt & McDougall, 1994) and international strategies of small firms (Baird, Lyles & Orris, 1994; Birley & Westhead, 1994; Namiki, 1988) and effect of small firm size in exporting (D'Souza & Eramilli, 1993; Calof, 1993). However no studies comparing differences across small companies based on age have been conducted to date.

On the other hand, the International Marketing literature boasts hundreds of studies on small business exporting that investigate motives for exporting (Cavusgil & Nevin, 1984), differences between exporters and non-exporters (Cavusgil & Naor, 1987; Miesenbock, 1988), the stages of internationalization (Johanson & Vahlne, 1977; Czinkota & Johnson, 1981; Sullivan & Bauerschmidt, 1990), and the role of management in the export decision (Ursic & Czinkota, 1984). These studies show that motives vary depending on attitude or demographics of the manager, firm specific advantages, or environmental context. While age has been included as a descriptive variable for sample characterization of exporters and non-exporters, it has not been the focus of any research.

In sum, no studies have considered possible differences in motives for internationalization that may result from age of the business. This is an important gap. Greater operating experience is associated with access to information and resources (Johanson & Vahlne, 1977). This may not only facilitate internationalization, but also lead to different international objectives. New and established small businesses differ across several dimensions, including the role of the owner/manager, structure and systems, experience in the industry, and focus (Churchill & Lewis, 1983). Therefore it is reasonable to expect that there may be significant differences between companies that internationalize at different ages, having implicaitons for strategy, international objectives and ultimately for performance. In other words, timing of entry into international markets may affect the type of strategy and performance of the small business (Eisenhardt, 1990).

Collectively, theories from International Business suggest that companies will internationalize after achieving a firm advantage, establishing market position, or as a result of industry structure dynamics. Theories rooted in organizational behavior propose that firms will internationalize in incremental steps as they have gained market experience (Aharoni, 1966; Cavusgil & Nevin, 1981; Johanson & Vahlne, 1977). Theories emanating from industrial economics posit that investment abroad occurs only after a domestic market position has been established (Buckley, 1983). Designed to explain foreign direct investment of multinational enterprises (MNE's), it is assumed a company is large and experienced, not adequately explaining reasons why new small companies might internationalize.

Theories from Entrepreneurship explain why new ventures might be created, or how small companies may be entrepreneurial. This literature focuses on four main dimensions; risk-bearing, innovation, general management and creation (Sandberg, 1992). Entrepreneurial theories are intended to explain individual entrepreneurial behavior; the venture creation process; or environmental factors contributing to entrepreneurship (Gartner, 1985; Bygrave & Hofer, 1991). These theories do not specifically address international behaviors, this research emphasizing domestic behaviors and activities, although arguably internationalization is entrepreneurial behavior.

Hence, no single theory of entrepreneurship or international business fully explains internationalization of new small companies. However, recent work by McDougall (1989); Oviatt & McDougall (1994); and McDougall, Shane & Oviatt (1994) offers a starting point. Their case study research on "global start-ups" defines an "international new venture" as a "business organization that from inception seeks to derive significant competitive advantages from the use of resources and sale of outputs in multiple countries". This work represents a first step in recognizing the international geographic scope of new ventures, even though this definition captures only a narrow segment of internationalized entrepreneurial businesses; those seeking competitive advantages through exchanges in multiple countries.

Exhibit #I.1 reflects boundaries of current theory. This exhibit uses two dimensions to illustrate the focus of theories and research; geographic scope of operations and organizational behaviors. The continuum, administrative—entrepreneurial, is widely accepted in entrepreneurship (Stevenson & Gumpert, 1985). Arguably, firms behaving in an entrepreneurial manner are more often new and/or small, being characterized as opportunity seeking, loosely structured and guided by the owner/founder (Churchill & Lewis, 1983). In contrast, administrative behavior is more often characteristic of large and old companies, described as hierarchical, powerful and planning driven (Stevenson & Gumpert, 1985). Exhibit #I.1 shows that entrepreneurial research and theories focus on quadrant #1; general business strategy research and theories emphasize quadrant #3; and international business theories and research center on quadrant #4. The domain of "international entrepreneurship", quadrant #2 is largely unexplored. This study, which explores international activities of companies based on age at internationalization, will focus on quadrant #2.

Exhibit #I.1
DOMAIN OF INTERNATIONAL ENTREPRENEURSHIP

GEOGRAPHIC SCOPE OF OPERATIONS [1]

	DOMESTIC	INTERNATIONAL
ENTREPRENURIAL	1 ENTREPRENEURSHIP	2 INTERNATIONAL ENTREPRENEURSHIP
ADMINISTRATIVE	3 BUSINESS STRATEGY	4 INTERNATIONAL BUSINESS (MNE)

ORGANIZATIONAL BEHAVIOR [2]

[1] Adapted from presentation by Brush, in McDougall, Oviatt and Brush, (1991)

[2] This continuum of behavior was proposed by Stevenson and Gumpert (1985)

DESCRIPTION OF RESEARCH

This research contributes to knowledge in the domain of international entrepreneurship. The effect of age on motives for internationalization in small businesses was investigated. Resulting international strategies and performance outcomes depending on age at internationalization also were studied. The context for this research was a national sample of 134 small (<500 employees) internationalized U.S. manufacturers. As noted earlier, new and established companies differ across certain dimensions. It was expected these differences would be evidenced in internationalized new and established small companies. This exploratory study identifies factors that caused these companies to go international; compares similarities and differences depending on early or late internationalization; and tests applicability of theoretical variables from international business and entrepreneurship explaining this phenomenon. Four questions guided this study:

1. What factors motivate young small businesses to engage in international business activities?

2. What factors motivate old small businesses to engage in international business activities?

3. Do reasons for internationalization vary significantly by age of small businesses?

4. Do international strategies vary by age of small business?

The answers to these questions have important implications. Because the role of the founder, resources, structures, systems and goals vary depending on the age of the business, internationalization at an early age may pose risks to these businesses by constraining resources. Conversely, late internationalization may result in missed opportunities. Similarly, variations in internationalization resulting from age may imply different assistance needs. For instance, companies selling abroad at a young age may need training and skill development, whereas companies internationalizing later in life may have a greater need for information.

Because general theories of international business were not intended to specifically explain the motives of small businesses, nor were theories of entrepreneurship designed to explain why they internationalize, this research integrates theories from both fields. According to mid-range theory development (Merton, 1962), this approach is appropriate for guiding empirical inquiry intermediate to general theories, and specific classes of social behavior. Therefore, the intent of this project is to determine if the variables from general theories about international business and entrepreneurship can be integrated in a framework which will enlighten us as to the international activities of small businesses.

A conceptual framework was developed by examining the theories and empirical works of entrepreneurship and international business. There are five main constructs in this framework; Contextual Factors, International Strategy, Performance, Regional Environment Conditions, and Host Country Conditions (see Exhibit II.2). Variables operationalizing these constructs were identified from empirical research and pilot studies in this project. Contextual Factors are composed of management, firm and industry variables that are theorized or empirically shown to be important to the decision to internationalize (Buckley & Casson, 1978; Morrison & Roth, 1989; Akhter & Friedman, 1989). International Strategy variables include modes of foreign market entry, export, licensing or contracting, or foreign direct investment (Morrison & Roth, 1989; Contractor, 1990); and degree of internationalization, geographic scope (Cavusgil, 1984; McDougall, 1989); and commitment of resources (Cavusgil, 1982; Vernon, 1983). The outcome result of contextual factors and strategy is performance which is defined as progress towards a goal of overall or international growth in sales or employees (Geringer, Beamish & daCosta, 1989; D'Souza & Eramilli, 1991).

Two sets of conditions influence these constructs; Regional Environment Conditions, which include local economic, political-regulatory, competitive, and demographic variables (Johanson & Vahlne, 1977; Buckley & Casson, 1978), and as Host Country Conditions, which are composed of economic, political-regulatory, cultural, and competitive variables (Goodnow & Hansz, 1972; Mascarenhas, 1986).

Using the conceptual framework developed as a basis for this research, (see Exhibit #I.2), the objective of this exploratory study was to develop a descriptive scheme and explore possible relationships between variables (Denzin, 1978). This research identifies which factors were important in the decision to sell products abroad. It describes how small

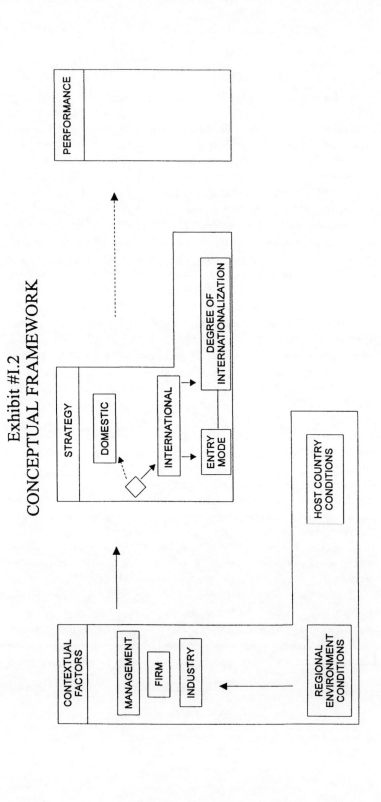

Exhibit #I.2
CONCEPTUAL FRAMEWORK

businesses implement international strategies and compares companies by age at internationalization. Performance outcomes were measured descriptively, but were not the main focus of this study. Even though it is recognized that importing activities are very important to small businesses and the balance of U.S. international trade, in order to narrow the scope of this project internationalization, defined as "receiving revenues from abroad" (see endnote number one), excludes discussion of importing activities.

The research design selected was a cross sectional survey, which is suitable for exploratory investigations of a phenomenon and allows for comparisons across two groups. Similarities and differences in motives and international strategies between young and old aged businesses at time of internationalization were hypothesized and tested statistically using descriptive statistics, correlation analyses, and discriminant function analysis.

DEFINITIONS

To facilitate the discussion of this research, it is important to clarify key terms that are used hereinafter. A theoretical and operational definition of each of the major terms is included in the following discussion.

There is a lack of consistency in the terminology used to discuss international business activities. The most frequently employed terms are "international strategy" (Eglehoff, 1988; Daniels, Pitts & Tretter, 1984) and "international business strategy" (Daniels, 1983) both of which can encompass international expansion (Mascarenhas, 1986), international diversification (Geringer, et al, 1989), exporting strategy (Miesenbock, 1988) and other alternative modes of international business activities such as "licensing" or "joint venturing" (Contractor, 1990). In the Entrepreneurship area, studies of international activities of small businesses generally refer to exporting strategy (Namiki, 1988) or joint ventures (D'Souza & McDougall, 1989). The terms "exporting" and "investing abroad" are too limiting when considering small companies. Consequently, unless otherwise specified this research will use the word "internationalize" to mean "to receive revenues from abroad from international business activities" (*Massachusetts International Export Service Guide*, 1989; *Dun's World Marketing Directory*, 1991). Another expression that will be used is "to enter foreign markets" (D'Souza & Eramilli, 1991); this being consistent with the theoretical definition of international business activities, means "resource exchange across national boundaries" (Fayerweather, 1978).

"Internationalization process" is defined as the consequence of incremental adjustments to the changing conditions of the firm and its environment (Aharoni, 1966). The process is conceived of as stepwise where the firm incrementally increases its international involvement over time (Johanson & Vahlne, 1977). As integration and use of knowledge about foreign markets and operations grows, commitment to foreign markets increases (Welch & Wiedersheim-Paul, 1980). Referred to as a "stage model", the internationalization process expands outward from home markets to those contiguous markets most compatible cognitively and in terms of resources and as market knowledge increases, commitment increases (Johanson & Vahlne, 1977; Welch & Loustarinen, 1988). This process is most frequently operationalized to describe exporting behavior. Typically there are between three and seven stages. The first stage is pre-involvement, middle stages are active involvement, and later stages are referred to as committed involvement (Cavusgil, 1984).

"International strategy" is defined as a pattern of objectives, policies, and plans for achieving goals (Aharoni, 1966, p. 294). International strategy is distinct from domestic strategy in that it includes international product/market dimensions (Daniels, 1983; Morrison & Roth, 1989). Operationalization of this term includes all options for foreign market entry (exporting, licensing and direct investment) (Caves, 1982; Contractor, 1990) and degree of internationalization (Cavusgil, 1984; Rugman, 1986). "Degree of internationalization" includes geographic scope of operations and commitment of resources. "Scope" is operationalized as number and diversity of countries and markets (Cavusgil, 1984). "Commitment" is defined as those dedicated assets that cannot be redeployed to alternative uses without loss of value (Vernon, 1983). Commitment can refer to social, financial, physical or human resources (Aharoni, 1966), and varies from low to high. This is operationalized as number of employees working abroad and percentage of total manufactured products sold abroad.

This research focuses on small businesses, which are defined as profit-oriented organizations in which there can rationally be only one profit center (McGuire, 1976). This is operationalized in accordance with U.S. Federal Government size breaks, and refers to businesses of less than 500 employees (*The State of Small Business*, 1990, p. 12; see footnote number two for further discussion).

"New businesses" are defined as organizations that are created by an individual or group of individuals for entry into a product/market (Gartner, 1985). In keeping with other research in the entrepreneurial area and government interpretation of new businesses, this will be operationalized as businesses of six or less years old (Kirchoff & Phillips, 1988; Fredriksen, et al 1989; *The State of Small Business*, 1989).

OVERVIEW

This book describes in detail the investigation of age in the internationalization of small companies. In Chapter I, I present the context for this research, describing the importance of small companies, international activities of new small companies, and differences between new and established businesses. Chapter II covers the theories of international business, and entrepreneurship. The chapter concludes with a discussion of theory integration. Chapter IV reviews and summarizes empirical literature related to small business internationalization. Chapter V describes the methodology and research design used for this study, and presents preliminary findings from pilot interviews. Data analysis and results are discussed in Chapter VI, while discussion of findings and answers to research questions are presented in Chapter VII. The last chapter offers conclusions and implications from this research.

NOTES

1. The term "internationalize 'is defined as' to receive revenues from abroad from international business activities"; *Massachusetts International Export Service Guide*, 1989; *Dun's World Marketing Directory*, 1991. This definition is consistent with Fayerweather, 1978, "resource exchange across national boundaries".

2. "Small businesses" are defined as those small and medium-sized businesses with less than 500 employees. This is consistent with standard business employment asset and receipt size classes established by the Office of Management and Budget used by all federal

agencies (*The State of Small Business*, 1989, p. 18). The categories noted are the following:

very small	< 20	employees
small	20-99	employees
medium	100-499	employees
large	> 500	employees

The SBA typically refers to "small" businesses as those with less than 500 employees (indicating non-large) unless otherwise speci-fied. This operationalization will be used in this research. Other researchers have used this operationalization; Roy & Simpson (1981), Witner (1980).

3. "New businesses" are defined as organizations created by an individual or group of individuals for entry into a product/market (Gartner, 1985). Consistent with the SBA and other researchers, new businesses will be operationalized as those companies six or less years of age (Kirchoff & Phillips, 1988; Fredricksen, et al, 1987; *The State of Small Business*, 1989).

Acknowledgments

This work began as my Dissertation. At the time, I never anticipated that so many people would contribute to its completion. I am very grateful to colleagues, business associates, friends and family who have helped me in this effort.

My work in Entrepreneurship began under the mentorship of Bob Hisrich who greatly influenced me to enter the Boston University School of Management Doctoral Program and subsequently to do this research. I am appreciative of his support and thoughtful advice. I thank Ted Murray, chair person of my committee, who generously offered guidance, creative suggestions and editorial ideas that greatly improved this project. Pieter VanderWerf and Sushil Vachani, members of my committee, helped by asking insightful questions and offering practical advice concerning the content and process of this research.

I am deeply indebted to the small business owners that completed the research questionnaires and willingly spent time to share information about their businesses making this investigation possible. I hope in some small way the results of my research will be useful to them.

Several colleagues offered suggestions and guidance during various phases of this project. In particular I thank Jim Post for helping me navigate throughout this lengthy research process, and Paul Berger who reviewed the statistical analysis sections of this study. Several Boston University faculty patiently read drafts, listened to presentations and offered comments. For these efforts, I thank Liam Fahey, John Mahon, John Russell, Steve Davidson, Melissa Stone, Jules Schwartz, Ken Hatten, Tomas Kohn, Fred Foulkes, Clif Smith and Wendy Greenfield.

I am appreciative of the assistance I received from Mike Peters, Barbara Bigelow, Dennis Ray and Don Sexton for ideas on research design and questionnaire development. Ben Oviatt and Patricia McDougall were particularly helpful in offering suggestions about how to study this emerging area of interational entrepreneurship. Bruce Phillips of the Small Business Administration, Patricia Givens, Michael Campbell and Bill Williams also offered practical suggestions and advice.

Several doctoral students commented on my work. I especially thank Margarete Arndt, Victor Rosenberg, Ed Desmarais, Mohan Subramaniam, Dick James, Deborah Fain and Jerry Smith.

My research involved many financial expenses and this burden was lessened by the generous assistance of two agencies, Boston University's Entrepreneurial Management Institute and the Richard D. Irwin Foudation Doctoral Dissertation Fellowship. I am grateful for their support.

As with any major research project, there are numerous administrative tasks, including editorial, printing, keypunching and word processing activities. I thank Diane McHegen, HeaLi Park, Jerry Neef, Matthew Martin, Sarah Brown, Sandra Kelleher, Kathryn Lopes, Mary Jennings, Karen Barry, Christine Moore, Kimberly Malec and Susan Traft.

Many of my friends offered continual support and encouragement. For this I thank Pat Coogan, Linda Hutton, Peter Hutton, and Barbara Bird. I am also grateful to the following people for caring for my children; Michele McDonald, Debbie O'Glishen, Jeanne McAteer, Caroline Archer, Tracey Stapel, Julia Hardy, Renee Benoit and Sarah Brown.

I owe the biggest debt for their support, unwavering confidence and tolerance to my family. My mother, Julie Greer, offered moral support and instilled in me a love of learning. My father, Barney Greer, inspired me with his entrepreneurial spirit. From start to finish, my daughters, Julie, Lucy and Emily, lived this project with me. Not only did they stuff envelopes and sort them by state, but they knew when to "leave Mom alone". I am grateful to Julie for being a good listener and inspiring me to work hard by showing her dedication to gymnastics. Lucy's passion for her horseback riding was similarly inspirational. Emily set a good example through her endurance in swimming and skating.

My final and most important thank you is to my husband David. He has encouraged me, expressed unwavering confidence in my ability, and offered moral support that exceeds expectations. Furthermore, he gave me the time to write by taking over many household tasks and driving, activities that are so much a part of our lives. Without his love and support, none of this would ever have been possible.

International
Entrepreneurship

I
Small Business and International Activities

"Record numbers of small businesses are turning overseas to bolster their profits ... 'Its an awakening', says Howard Lewis, vice-president of the National Association of Manufacturers, 'small companies are finding there is life beyond the domestic market'."(*Wall Street Journal*, November 8, 1990, p. B-2)

Small companies are increasingly active in international markets. Believing that there are growth opportunities abroad for smaller firms, the U.S. government is encouraging international trade in this segment. To provide context for this research, this chapter describes the current state of small business international activity and presents information about the role of new companies in the U.S. economy. A discussion of differences between new and established small companies is presented to provide a better understanding of the potential variation in international behaviors based on age of small business. It is expected these distinctions will explain variations in motives for early or late internationalization and resultant strategies.

INTERNATIONAL TRADE ACTIVITY

Small businesses are actively participating in international business activity. While the U.S. government does not collect statistics on international trade by size or age of enterprise,[1] there are a range of estimates, all suggesting increases in small business internationalization. In 1980, the Department of Commerce estimated that approximately 15,000 businesses having less than 500 employees received revenues from exports; these businesses accounting for about twenty to twenty-five percent of all exports (Rabino, 1980).

In 1988, the SBA estimated that 90,000 small firms exported to foreign markets, and that those with less than 100 employees accounted

3

for approximately twenty-five percent of the total or 22,500 enterprises (*Small Business in the American Economy*, 1988, p. 6). This estimate is close to a *Wall Street Journal* report (Nov. 8, 1990) that of 100,000 U.S. companies exporting, 80 percent are very small (less than 100 employees). Similarly, David Birch of Cognetics Inc., announced that more than eighty-seven percent of the 51,000 exporters tracked by his company employed fewer than 500 employees (*Business Week*, April 13, 1992, p. 70). For the year 1989, exports by small companies were up 11.1 percent from 1988, compared to imports which rose 6.1 percent, resulting in a decline in the foreign trade deficit (*The State of Small Business*, 1990, p. xi).

Sample surveys of small businesses also reflect growth in internationalization by small companies. A recent study by Dun and Bradstreet found that of small and medium-sized firms (less than 500 employees), forty-one percent of respondents reported export sales growth rate above domestic sales growth rate, and these firms accounted for 25.7 percent of all exports by firms with less than 100 employees (Holziger, Dec. 1990a). An investigation of the U.S. Department of Commerce PIERS data base found that firms of less than 500 employees accounted for approximately twelve percent of the value of direct export by manufacturing firms (Faucett, 1985). Exports accounted for approximately nineteen percent of growth in GNP in 1989, with small businesses contributing about twenty percent of the total U.S. exports. Results of a recent survey by the National Association of Manufacturers of 2,105 of its 8,200 small manufacturers found a twelve percent growth in businesses receiving revenues from exporting. Increases measured up from fifty-four percent in 1988 to sixty-six percent in 1992 (Braunlich, 1992). Furthermore, government officials predicted that the number of small companies exporting will increase in the future.

There are several factors contributing to this increase in international trade by small companies. These include political and economic changes; a successful conclusion to negotiations of the General Agreement on Tarrifs and Trade (GATT) and the North American Free Trade Agreement (NAFTA); a favorable U.S. policy position on international trade; and greater availability of resources to small companies.

Dramatic changes in the world economy with the opening of markets in countries such as the Czech Republics, Hungary, former Soviet Union and Vietnam, have created new opportunities for small companies. Dun and Bradstreet suggests that the political and economic changes in Eastern Europe will encourage even greater international trade among smaller businesses (Holziger, 1990b, Holziger, 1990c). In addition, growing economies in many developing countries present new market opportunities for small companies. Argentina and China are two examples of countries where GNP growth is projected, and economic reforms have created more spending power for their citizens (Maynard, 1994).

Successful negotiations on trade agreements are another factor contributing to increased opportunites for small businesses. As of January 1994 NAFTA was implemented, eliminating trade barriers among the U.S., Mexico and Canada, and designed to be particularly helpful to small companies. Coincidently, this year marks the successful conclusion of the Uruguay round of GATT. This agreement is expected to reduce and eliminate tariffs among the 117 signatories beginning in 1995. According to Lawrence Chimerine, Chief Economist and Vice President of the Economic Statistics Institute for Small Companies, "The opportunities [for small companies] to export are better now than the have been in a long time..." (Maynard, 1994, p. 23).

Besides these developments in international markets, the U.S. government is encouraging greater participation in international trade by small businesses: "One important mission of the U.S. Small Business Administration is to encourage small and medium-sized firms to export their products to other nations" (*Small Business in the American Economy*, 1988, p. iii). Three reasons are given for this position. First, to improve the balance of trade—U.S. small businesses import more than they export, especially in the retail and wholesale trade sectors (*Small Business in the American Economy*, 1988). Second, to survive—if small businesses are to participate more fully in the development of the American economy between now and the year 2000, a major area of engagement must be the international economy (*Small Business in the American Economy*, 1988, p. 23). Third, there are opportunities—from now to 1996 the world economy is expected to grow at an average rate of 3.3 percent per year, whereas the domestic economy is expected to grow only at an average rate of 2.4 percent (*Small Business in the American Economy*, 1988, p. 23). Furthermore, dollar exchange rates have declined, making it more cost-effective for small businesses to do business internationally (*Small Business in the American Economy*, 1988, p. 25).

The U.S. government also is assisting small companies threatened by foreign competition in domestic markets. In 1993, 249 small companies received trade adjustment assistance providing consulting, grants and other aid to help small companies recover from import "injury". The total financial assistance was approximately $10 million for this year (Sullivan, 1994).

Even though the Small Business Administration is quite clear about its position encouraging small businesses to internationalize, and there are at least fifteen to eighteen separate federal agencies involved in promotion of exporting. These agencies seldom coordinate activities with each other (*Wall Street Journal*, March 5, 1992, p. B-2; *Business Week*, April 13, 1992, p. 70). For example, The SBA and the Commerce Department both offer counseling and market information through a network of offices and also sponsor overseas trade missions.

Another factor affecting increases in international trade are developments in communications and greater availability of resources and assistance. Improvements in telecommunications, such as FAX machines, 800 telephone numbers and overnight express mail, also have helped to make international markets more accessible to small firms (*Business Week*, April 13, 1992, p. 70). Likewise information is more widely available form export assistance centers (one stop shops) in major cities such as Baltimore, Miami, Chicago, and Long Beach, Calif. (Maynard, 1994). Further, agencies such as the Japan External Trade Organization (JETRO) have been created to promote trade between Japan and small companies."No-one is too small to export"; says John Everett, Executive Vice President of Dage Company, an export management company located in Stamford, Conn. Like Dage company, there are many companies specializing in finding overseas markets for U.S. manufacturers.

In sum, many factors are contributing to a favorable climate for small companies to internationalize. Global market developments, a favorable U.S. public policy position, technological developments, and greater resource assistance have encouraged even very young companies to enter the international marketplace.

NEW BUSINESSES IN THE U.S ECONOMY

New businesses are important to the U.S. economy because they are a source of job creation (*Small Business in the American Economy*, 1988, p. 64-67) and innovations (Birch, 1987). A recent study by Kirchoff and Phillips (1988) found new businesses created a greater proportion of new jobs than established firms. New businesses also have been attributed with implementing more innovations than larger established firms (Birch, 1987). There is no single listing of new start-ups or new businesses, but several proxies are used: incorporations—compiled by Dun and

Bradstreet;[2] self-employed, compiled by the Department of Labor,[3] and Small Businesses for which information is maintained by the Small Business Administration. According to these proxy lists, best estimates are that approximately 600,000 new small businesses are created every year (*Small Business in the American Economy*, 1988, pp. 64-65; *The State of Small Business*, 1989, p. 23; *The State of Small Business*, 1990, p. xii). For the year 1991, the SBA estimated there were 734,304 start-ups, down 6.6 percent from the record 786,056 for 1990.

Despite the numbers of businesses created, many new small businesses are discontinued for one reason or another. While there is again no complete listing of business failures or discontinuances, the rate of business closings has been estimated by the SBA. In 1988, there were about 63,000 recorded small company bankruptcies and 57,000 failures. This represents about 10 percent of all small companies leaving the marketplace due to financial and non-financial reasons. In addition, between 1988-1990 there were 7.8 million jobs lost due to business dissolutions, and 9.2 million jobs created through business births during this period according to the Small Business Administration's small business data base (Phillips, 1993). Among growing firms (those that add new jobs), approximately eight percent close within the first two years compared to approximately thirty percent of those small businesses that do not grow (*The State of Small Business*, 1989, p. 22). In the first six years, the overall discontinuance rate is estimated at approximately 62.7 percent for small businesses. However, for growing firms the rate is again significantly lower, 33.7 percent versus 72.5 percent for businesses that do not grow (*The State of Small Business*, 1989, p. 22). In other words, for new small businesses to survive, growth and expansion by adding jobs are of major importance. One means of growth is engaging in international business activity.

INTERNATIONAL ACTIVITY AND NEW COMPANIES

The U.S. government does not keep track of international business activity by age of business.[4] Yet, there is some information to indicate that small businesses often export at an early age. For example, a recent article from the *Wall Street Journal* described the international activities of the Brooklyn Brewery, started in 1988, and its arrangements to export its beer to Japan. Foreign sales accounted for about ten percent of the Brewery's two million dollars in annual sales (*Wall Street Journal*, Oct. 13, 1990). Other popular publications have highlighted international success stories of businesses that begin by selling products abroad at an early age. Examples include Garber Floor Testing, a six year old enterprise that sold its devices in England before entering U.S. markets (*Nation's Business*, September, 1991, p.8). The case of Quantum Epitaxial Designs, Inc. is similar. Quantum, started in 1988, worked with a Pennsylvania state program called Ben Franklin Technology Partnership to obtain venture funding and sell its crystallized wafers to Japan (*Nation's Business*, July, 1991, p. 9). Similarly, there is LIFE Corporation, a twelve employee firm founded in 1985, that started exporting in 1987. The company, which makes a portable oxygen pac, now receives more than forty percent of its revenues from foreign countries (*Business America*, June 3, 1991, p. 21). Barnyard Babies, a toy manufacturer also sold products to Japan, France, Brazil and Canada within its first three years of operations; and Cottage Country Baskets, a manufacturer of handcrafted baskets, also exported from inception.

In summary, there is data new small businesses are important to our economy. Furthermore, anecdotal evidence suggests new companies from various industrial sectors are selling abroad to many different countries. Despite this evidence of growth in internationalized new ventures, there is neither a count of the number of new small businesses that are internationalized, nor information about their reasons for, or experiences in internationalization. There also is reason to believe companies internationalizing early in life rather than late will differ because of the inherent differences between new and established small businesses.

DIFFERENCES BETWEEN NEW AND ESTABLISHED SMALL BUSINESSES

The main premise of this research is the acknowledged differences between new and established (young and old) small businesses. It is believed these differences will be evidenced in their approaches to internationalization. Strong support for this presumption exists in the entrepreneurship literature. While it has been shown that not all organizations follow the same developmental cycle (Churchill & Lewis, 1983; Eggers, Leahy & Churchill, 1994) there are characteristic differences between newly created and established small companies, the most obvious difference being life span (Grenier, 1972). Besides this, there are four primary dimensions across which new and established small businesses differ. These are (1) the role of the manager, (2) resources, (3) organizational structure and systems, and (4) focus (see Exhibit #1.1).

First, the role of the manager is a dimension that varies by age of company. While the manager is generally prominent in small companies due to fewer employees, in new companies the manager is often the founder and therefore is more crucial and dominant. As noted by Churchill and Lewis, "The owner does everything and directly supervises subordinates...the owner is the business, performs all important tasks, and is the major supplier of energy, direction, and, with relatives and friends, capital." (1983, p. 32). Other authors have noted that the identity of the firm is often that of the founder (Kao, 1989), and it is his/her skills and values that drive the firm (Cooper, 1981; Scott & Bruce, 1980; Bird, 1989). The owner/founder is critical in acquiring the resources, making decisions and motivating the employees, (Cooper, 1981; Marchesnay & Julien, 1990), often relying on personal connections, trust (Larson, 1992), and charisma rather than organizational competence or systems. Day to day activities and strategic direction are guided by the "vision" of the creator (Drucker, 1985) or his/her intuition rather than rational planning (Miller, 1983). Feeser and Willard (1990) investigated the effect of the founder's background (knowledge, skills, and occupational experience) on start-up strategy and concluded there was indeed a strong relationship between his/her background and early strategy of a new venture.

In contrast to the dominant role of the owner/founder in new ventures, in established small businesses the founder may no longer be present, and his/her role is less dominant. Churchill and Lewis (1983) suggest that the manager becomes dis-engaged, while Grenier (1972) noted managers in established small businesses more often delegate responsibilities. As Cooper notes, "Typically, the role of the founder changes, with 'doing' activities largely delegated and with the job becoming more managerial in character" (1981, p. 43).

Another example of variation in the role of the manager has to do with focus. In new ventures, owner/founders are typically concerned with seeking opportunities (Timmons, 1985; Bird, 1989), whereas in established small businesses the concern is for solving problems (Stevenson & Gumpert, 1985; Churchill & Lewis, 1983). Consistent with this, in new ventures the owner/founders seek to acquire resources rather than manage and control resources (Stevenson & Gumpert, 1985). In other words, the age of the business is related to the role the owner/founder assumes in the business (Grenier, 1972; Cooper, 1981; Churchill & Lewis, 1983).

Exhibit #1.1

DIFFERENCES BETWEEN NEW AND ESTABLISHED
SMALL BUSINESSES

Dimension	Characteristics of New Small Businesses	Characteristics of Established Small Businesses
1- Manager's Role	dominant, is often founder, skills and values drive firm (Cooper, 1981; Kao, 1989; Feeser & Willard, 1990)	manager is dis-engaged, (Churchill & Lewis, 1983) involved in general activities and planning (Deeks,1972)
	concern with seeking opportunities (Stevenson & Gumpert, 1985, Timmons, 1985; Bird, 1989)	concern with solving problems (Churchill & Lewis, 1983)
	acquires resources (Stevenson & Gumpert, 1985)	manages and controls resources (Stevenson & Gumpert, 1985)
2- Resources	limited capital, personal rather than borrowed (Stevenson & Gumpert 1985; Cooper & Dunkelberg, 1986)	capital available, often borrowed (Cooper, 1982)
	few employees perform multiple tasks, knowledge and skills may be limited (Cooper & Dunkelberg, 1986)	experienced employees have defined tasks (Cooper, 1982)
Organizational 3a- Structure	loose and flexible (Churchill & Lewis, 1983; Kazanjian & Drazin, 1990; Vesper, 1990)	administrative structure in place (Churchill & Lewis, 1983)
3b- Systems	minimal and evolving, little or no planning takes place (Churchill & Lewis, 1983; Sexton & Van Auken, 1984)	established systems, planning frequently occurs (Churchill & Lewis, 1983; Eggers, Leahy & Churchill, 1994)
	individualistic and intuitive decisionmaking (Miller, 1983)	established pattern of decision-making (Churchill & Lewis, (1983)
4- Focus	existence, survival and attaining legitimacy (Lippit & Schmidt, 1967; Churchill & Lewis, 1983)	how to change- expand or grow, adapting to environment, achieving uniqueness (Lippit & Schmidt, 1967; Churchill & Lewis, 1983)
	developing viable product/service and customer base (Eggers, Leahy & Churchill, 1994)	developing internal systems to meet demands of growth (Eggers, Leahy & Churchill, 1994)

A second dimension that often distinguishes new and established companies is resources. While it has been noted that all small businesses are typically more resource constrained than large firms, among small businesses new ventures face greater difficulties than established small firms in acquiring capital, skilled labor, and facilities (Churchill & Lewis, 1983; Cooper & Dunkelberg, 1986). New ventures lack experience and reputation in the marketplace, which limits their ability to borrow funds. Hence, they are typically financed with personal capital or loans from family or friends (Churchill & Lewis, 1983; Kazanjian 1988). This is referred to as a liability of newness (Stinchcombe, 1965); where young organizations are at a disadvantage due to lack of experience in their roles as social actors and lack of legitimacy which restricts their access to capital, materials and labor markets.

In addition to being capital constrained, new ventures have fewer employees that often must perform multiple tasks (Churchill & Lewis, 1983). Because the new small business suffers from a lack of experience, employees may not have clearly defined tasks, whereas in an established small business, these will be better defined (Cooper, 1981; Churchill & Lewis, 1983).

The third area where new and established small businesses differ is in their organizational structures and systems. Newer businesses tend to have loose and flexible structures (Churchill & Lewis, 1983; Kazanjian & Drazin, 1990) sometimes referred to as hybrid (Vesper, 1990). On the other hand, in established businesses, there is a more clearly defined chain of command, or hierarchy (Grenier, 1972; Churchill & Lewis, 1983). Studies describe new ventures as extremely informal and unstructured (Van de Ven, et al, 1984; Flamholtz, 1986).

Besides differences in organizational structures, the internal systems in new small businesses are comparatively minimal and informal (Churchill & Lewis, 1983; Gibb & Scott, 1985), and the decision-making systems in new ventures tend to be more centralized (Grenier, 1972). Characteristically, little planning is conducted by new small businesses (Frank, Plaschka & Roessl, 1989; Sexton & Van Auken, 1984; Robinson & Pearce, 1984; Spitzer, Alpar & Hills, 1989), this at best being cash forecasting (Churchill & Lewis, 1983). Moreover strategy making in "...simple firms tends to be intuitive rather than analytical...there is generally little planning, time horizons are short and they focus on operating matters" (Miller & Friesen, 1984, p. 179). Flamholtz (1986) describes systems in new ventures as "free spirited" in nature.

In contrast, organizational systems in established small businesses are more clearly defined, functional areas have been developed, and decision-making is often more decentralized (Churchill & Lewis, 1983; Eggers, Leahy & Churchill, 1994). Production, marketing, and financial systems are in place and this allows the business to focus on expansion or growth. While planning may not be formal, as in the case of large established organization, planning is used as a means to identify problems and to evaluate the implications of current strategy (Cooper, 1981) and to gain acquisition to financial resources (Hustedde & Pulver, 1992).

Finally, the fourth area of difference is focus. New ventures are typically focused on existence or survival, whereas established ventures are concerned with how to change (Lippit & Schmidt, 1967). The new small business is concerned with attaining legitimacy. New ventures typically emphasize development of a viable product/service and definable customer base which will lead to continued survival and legitimacy (Eggers, Leahy & Churchill, 1994). In contrast, established small firms work to develop a reputation, achieve uniqueness, adapt to the environment, or contribute to society (Lippit & Schmidt, 1967; Churchill & Lewis, 1983; Kazanjian & Drazin, 1990). Established small organizations have achieved legitimacy, and therefore emphasize development of management and internal systems to meed the demands of growth (Eggers, Leahy & Churchill, 1994).

These distinctions between new and established businesses suggest the existence of variations in approaches to internationalization. The decision to sell a product abroad at a young age would be conditioned by the minimal operating experience, and the characteristics associated with new firms. On the other hand, the decision of an established business to internationalize would be made in the context of a track record of operating experience. It is expected that these distinct characteristics of new and established small businesses will affect their motives for internationalization and types of international strategies.

SUMMARY

Record numbers of small businesses are active participants in international markets. One segment of companies receiving revenues from abroad are new small businesses. These new small businesses are important to the U.S. economy because they are major contributors of new jobs and innovations. While, there is no accurate government accounting of internationalized new ventures, there are many published cases of small businesses that have internationalized in their first six years of exististence.

The existence of four major distinctions between new and established small businesses; (the role of the manager, resources, structure and systems, and focus) implies differences in reasons for internationalization and resultant strategies. Furthermore, it is likely that the timing of international market entry depending on age may result in certain performance advantages or disadvantages. The next chapter will discuss theories of internationalization and their application to new and established small companies.

NOTES

1. An "enterprise" is a business organization consisting of one or more establishments under the same ownership or control (*The State of Small Business,* 1989, p. 21, footnote no. 4, p. 188).

2. Lists of incorporations are compiled by Dun and Bradstreet as proxies for newly created businesses. These listings account for about 80 percent of all revenues and are obtained from Secretary of State's Offices. These incorporations may mean intent to start, actual starts, changes in geographic location, or conversion of partnerships or sole proprietorships to incorporated enterprises (*Small Business in the American Economy*, 1988, p. 22).

3. Self-employed enterprises are those businesses that have no employees (*The State of Small Business*, 1989, p. 18).

4. Foreign trade statistics are collected by product class, weight, and average value. No data is collected by size of firm, but the Office of Advocacy, a division of the Small Business Administration, is working to produce such information using PIERS data collected and published by the *Journal of Commerce* (*Small Business in the American Economy*, 1988, p. 25, footnote).

II
Theoretical Background

There is extensive literature from international business explaining why firms will internationalize. Although there are several theories, two distinct streams are evident. The first stream is rooted in organizational behavior. These theories suggest that organizational decision-making will guide the choice to internationalize, describing the process as incremental or a stage model. The second stream is based on industrial economics which argues that market structures, and competitive industry dynamics will motivate internationalization. Intended to explain the foreign direct investment of multi-national enterprises, economics based theories do not distinguish between businesses by size or age. On the other hand, theories of entrepreneurship explain venture creation and entrepreneurial activities of small companies but focus on domestic activities. Therefore an integration of theories from international business and entrepreneurship is proposed as a guide to further understanding of small company internationalization.

BEHAVIORAL THEORIES OF INTERNATIONALIZATION

Behavioral theories assume that internationalization is an outcome of a sequential process of incremental adjustments to the changing conditions of the firm and its environment (Aharoni, 1966) (see Exhibit #2.1). The internationalization process describing the decision-making behavior of the organization is rooted in work by Cyert and March (1963) and Simon (1957). According to Cyert and March (1963), the major problem of the organization is environmental uncertainty which can be resolved incrementally as the organization gains experience, thereby accumulating standard procedures for resolving conflicts with the environment (Cyert & March, 1963). In other words, risk is reduced through experience or organizational learning.

Exhibit #2.1

GENERAL ASPECTS OF THEORIES
OF INTERNATIONAL BUSINESS

Behavioral Theories

Interpretation:	Internationalization is the outcome of a stepwise process designed to resolve uncertainty (Aharoni, 1966; Johanson & Vahlne, 1977) (explains exporting)
Goal:	To reduce risk and avoid uncertainty
Motivations:	Knowledge gained through experience Perceived threats or opportunities
Process:	Incremental and sequential; a stepwise process where risk and commitment increase as the organization gains more experience, or learns
Assumptions:	Business is going concern Sequential attention to goals Business has resources and capabilities to gather and evaluate information

Industrial Economics- Classical Theories

Interpretation:	A search for new exchange opportunities motivates international expansion (foreign investment) (Hymer, 1960)
Goal:	Profit maximization through efficient resource allocation
Motivations:	Limited exchange opportunities in home markets (domestic opportunities exploited) Intense competition in home markets Firm specific advantage; size or market position Industry maturity
Process:	Rational identification and assessment of exchange opportunities in home and domestic markets
Assumptions:	Business is going concern Market position is established Possession of resources and capabilities to gather information, evaluate and take advantage of international exchange opportunities Firms will have sufficient size

Exhibit # 2.1 (continued)

Industrial Economics- Neoclassical Theories

Interpretation:	Internationalization is the internalization of markets by diversification or integration, or foreign direct investment (Buckley & Casson, 1983)
Goal:	To achieve efficiency by decreasing risk and uncertainty, or safeguarding assets
Motivations:	Firm specific advantage — information, skills, technology, product, or resources Environmental uncertainty
Process:	Rational evaluation of transaction costs, and matching of costs to appropriate governance structure in either internal or external markets
Assumptions:	Companies have similar goals, primarily efficiency Businesses have the resources and capabilities to diversify or integrate Limited role of management; management and ownership are separated

Johanson and Vahlne (1977) employed Cyert and March's theory to explain export behavior. Domestic problems and environmental changes resulting in a perceived threat, such as higher cost of raw materials, or even non-economic factors, including socio-political or trade policies, might motivate a company to seek new suppliers abroad. The decision to export hinges on experiential learning. In their conception, "The better the knowledge about the market, the stronger the commitment" (Johanson & Vahlne, 1977, p. 28). Hence to avoid risks, a firm will expand outward from home markets to markets that are cognitively and geographically close before entering markets that are physically and culturally distant. For example, a U.S. company based in Montana would be more likely to export to Canada where English is spoken and the geographic distance is close, rather than to sell products to Turkey which is culturally different and a great distance away. This process of internationalization is conceived of as a stage model where commitment increases incrementally. Johanson and Vahlne (1977) view internationalization as a process in which firms gradually increase their international involvement as they gain experience.

Similar to Johanson and Vahlne, Aharoni (1966) views internationalization as a stepwise decision process. In explaining the foreign investment decision process, he describes specific steps: a decision to look, a decision to invest, and commitment to invest as characteristic of the process (Aharoni, 1966). Aharoni argues that Cyert and March's (1963) theory is limiting because it assumes decisions are only problem driven, avoids explicit discussion of environmental effects, and does not recognize the more powerful role of executive management. In his work, Aharoni (1966) notes that leadership factors provide internal impetus for internationalization and suggests external initiatives may be opportunity driven rather than reactions to problems. According to Aharoni (1966), the choice to invest abroad depends on the strength of the initiating force which can be either internal to the firm (executive drive), or external threats or opportunities.

Theories from International Marketing follow Johanson and Vahlne's (1977) view that the decision to export is the consequence of a process of incremental adjustments to the environment where commitment and risk increase at each stage of international involvement from pre-export to direct investment (Cavusgil, 1984). Similar to Johanson and Vahlne (1977), experience becomes a precondition for internationalization.

Recently theorists have proposed that businesses may not internationalize in sequential steps (Welch & Loustarinen, 1988) and that the stage model may be too deterministic (Melin, 1992). This work argues that firms may "leapfrog" or skip stages. There is little research to date that has investigated these ideas.

In sum, behavioral theories assume experiential learning precedes the decision to invest abroad (Aharoni, 1966) or export (Johanson & Vahlne, 1977; Cavusgil, 1984). Furthermore, international activity is defined as a consequence of incremental adjustments to the environment as experience and organizational learning accumulate. Similarly, it is assumed that businesses have the resource capabilities and organizational structures to search for information and identify opportunities or threats. Implicit in this assumption, is a size dimension, which probably arises because theories were developed based on research and inductions about large firms (Aharoni, 1966).

While not intended to distinguish among businesses by size or age, these behavioral theories adequately explain why established businesses, large or small, will decide to invest abroad (Aharoni, 1966) or export (Johanson & Vahlne, 1977; Cavusgil, 1984). It is logical that an older small business will have the structures and systems to identify and evaluate domestic threats or opportunities, which then may stimulate the collection of information about opportunities abroad, in turn resulting in a decision to internationalize. However, the presumption of a track record of experience, and the capability to collect information, evaluate opportunities and threats and implement international business activities would seem to disqualify these theories from application to young small ventures that frequently have few employees, lack market experiences, resources and established decision-making systems. Moreover, as noted earlier, new small ventures differ from established small businesses in that they characteristically have few resources (Churchill & Lewis, 1983), are structured informally (Vesper, 1990; Churchill & Lewis, 1983), and do not proceed in a planned fashion (Frank, Plaschka & Roessl, 1989). Furthermore, the notion of risk or uncertainty avoidance is contrary to the findings of entrepreneurial research where some level of risk-taking is generally agreed to be part of the venture creation process (See, Brockhaus, 1980; Kent, Sexton & Vesper, 1982; Bird, 1989; Gartner, 1985; Vesper, 1980). Because new ventures do not typically plan or avoid risk, these aspects of behavioral theories do not seem to apply.

On the other hand, there are factors in these theories that may apply. For example, bias towards the importance of managerial attitudes, and experience and knowledge (Aharoni, 1966; Reid, 1980) about the decision to export is consistent with the dominant role of the owner/-

founder in strategy-making in new ventures (Feeser & Willard, 1990; Holzmuller, & Kaspar, 1990; Cooper, 1981). Likewise, McMullan and Long (1990) and Bird (1989) refer to the importance of the vision of the entrepreneur in directing the new venture. Hence, Aharoni's contention that internal initiation to invest abroad may arise from the executive's pursuit of goals also may explain the internationalization motives of new ventures. Similarly, it could be argued that new small businesses may have experience in the form of business skills or industry knowledge acquired by the management team in their previous occupational and educational experiences (Cooper & Dunkelberg, 1986) that might be transferred to the new venture. Career experience may lead to management "expertise" (Bull & Willard, 1993) facilitating the learning experience and advancing the start-up process. Therefore, the experiential knowledge of the management may compensate for a lack of business operating experience allowing a young venture to export or invest from start-up. McDougall (1989) proposes this in her discussion of "international entrepreneurship" which she defines as start-ups that are internationalized from the beginning.

Another aspect of behavioral theory that may apply to new company internationalization is Aharoni's (1966) suggestion is that an external opportunity may present itself and motivate the business to invest abroad. In other words, companies will be encouraged to internationalize due to unsolicited orders or demand for products or services. A major premise of entrepreneurship theory is the pursuit of opportunity (Stevenson & Gumpert, 1985; Bygrave & Hofer, 1991). The entrepreneur identifies and takes advantage of an opportunity. As a motivation for exporting or investing abroad, perceptions of opportunities may well be a cause for young ventures to sell abroad. This argument is supported in recent work by McDougall, Shane & Oviatt (1994). Drawing from case studies of international new ventures, they suggest these founders are more "alert" to possibilities of combining resources from different markets because of competencies they have developed from their earlier activities.

In summary, behavioral theories suggest that businesses will internationalize in response to perceived threats or opportunities, which are internal or external to the firm. The process is characterized as logical and stepwise, where commitment and risk abroad increase as the organization gains operating experience and learns. Because these theories were intended to explain internationalization in established companies, they presume businesses have experience and plan incrementally, adequately applying to old small companies. However, these theories have not been tested for application to young small businesses. Even though the theoretical premises of risk avoidance, sequential planning, and operational experience do not always apply to new ventures, motives such as internal executive drive and pursuit of opportunities do to explain the decision to export or invest abroad in young firms.

INDUSTRIAL ECONOMICS THEORIES OF INTERNATIONALIZATION

Classical Theories

According to classical international economic theory, supply and demand drive international exchange activity. Firms, or groups of firms, seek to satisfy unfulfilled or imperfectly filled international exchange opportunities (Hymer, 1960) (see Exhibit #2.1). Internationalization, defined as foreign direct investment, occurs to fulfill an exchange opportunity. Classical theories were intended to explain the behavior of multinational enterprises (MNE's), defined as an enterprise which owns and controls assets in more than one country (Casson, 1979). These theories assume perfect competition and employ equilibrium concepts, equating multinational activity with capital arbitrage between countries (Caves, 1982). This stream of literature attempts to describe a fully integrated theory of investment, production, and distribution. The main motives for direct investment are to gain high returns (profits). The existence of factors of production (resources), low tariffs, large market size, and favorable exchange rates that can create scale economies or minimize costs, may encourage a firm to locate production abroad or to export.

Industry structure theories are rooted in the Bain (1968) paradigm that strategy follows structure. The structural conditions of the industry environment at home or in the host country are posited as the main factors contributing to the internationalization of the firm. A business facing intense competition, or mature industry conditions, will be likely to seek exchanges outside of domestic markets (Kothari, 1978). In other words, foreign investment may occur if costs in the host country are lower than in the home country. Relatedly, monopolistic advantage theory assumes that unique assets built in home markets, such as product differentiation, economies of scale, specific skills or market position are transferrable abroad (Kindleberger, 1969). Hence, in order to overcome the costs of doing business abroad, firms must possess some sort of advantage

(Hymer, 1960; Robock & Simmonds, 1983). This presumes the MNE exists because it has superior and non-replicable advantages over foreign firms (Caves, 1982). Because of these advantages, a firm can exploit its advantages overseas for a lower cost than in the home country.

Closely related to industry structure theories is the oligopolistic reaction theory. Knickerbocker (1973) points out that firms will become MNE's to match the actions of their competition, illustrated by similar timing of entry into certain markets. This imitative behavior reduces risk. In other words, internationalization will occur in reaction to actions by competition, with a goal of reducing risk (Buckley & Brooke, 1992).

Another theory offered as an explanation for the MNE is the product cycle theory (Vernon, 1966). Based on stages of product development, this theory suggests new products will appear in the most advanced countries. As the product is accepted and standardized, economies of scale will lead to expansion in production, increasing demand, and eventually low costs, which will motivate international sales. Recent work counters the assumptions of this model arguing it is too deterministic and that advanced countries may not always be the source of new product development (Buckley & Brooke, 1992).

Relatedly, theories of political economy propose a bargaining power model to explain the evolution of the MNE in developing countries (Kobrin, 1987; Vachani, 1991). The outcome of the bargaining relationship between the MNE and host country determines the level of ownership of the subsidiary. In this view, political imperatives can motivate foreign direct investment.

Dunning (1988) integrates key firm attributes or advantages, with country and industry factors to explain MNE activity in a holistic framework, referred to as the eclectic paradigm. This paradigm notes the importance of organizational activities and advantages in the internationalization decision. More recently, the concept of firm advantage has been questioned (Buckley, 1983) due to assumptions about size and information barriers (Teece, 1983).

Taken together, classical theories assume that international exchange opportunities exist, and that the MNE is a going enterprise. The reasons for internationalization arise largely from industry structural and market conditions rather than individual managerial factors. By definition, a MNE is of large size, is established and possesses market power (Caves, 1982). These advantages will allow it to take advantage of international opportunities. On the other hand, a firm lacking in scale economies, absolute cost control, and production differentiation (Dunning, 1974) can only adapt because it is dominated by its environment.

These classical theories provide explanations for direct investment of large oligopolistic firms with substantial size, market power, and resources. Companies with these advantages, when confronted with market saturation or intense domestic competition, have the ability to identify and exploit exchange opportunities abroad thereby maximizing their profits. In the case of smaller firms, they lack these size and power advantages, leading to a lack of market confidence typically manifested by a higher cost of capital. This in turn, results in fewer resources (Casson, 1983) restricting international expansion capability. More specifically, it has been noted that large firm size and foreign direct investment go hand-in-hand (Caves, 1982, p. 71).

According to these theories, small businesses, either new or established, will be unable to succeed internationally because of their size disadvantage. Small businesses are restricted in their ability to expand internationally because they lack the resources to gather and evaluate information about international opportunities (Mascarenhas, 1986) and to implement strategies of direct investment (Kindleberger, in Dunning, 1970)

New small businesses are not only constrained by size but also by a lack of market experience, or "liability of newness" (Stinchcombe, 1965). Furthermore, their industry position has not been established because their market acceptance is still uncertain. Hence, motives for internationalization arising from on oligopolistic market position, limited domestic market opportunity, or a need to meet the reaction of competitors, do not adequately explain exporting or direct investment in small firms.

Conversely, small firms have some advantages over large firms in exporting to overseas markets. They can be more flexible in meeting market demands and react more quickly to prevailing market forces (Pezeshkpur, 1979). While foreign governments may offer incentives for companies to invest or import, large firms may forgo smaller market opportunities. For instance, large firms may consider recently opened European markets too small, or difficult to reach, instead concentrating on Western European markets where markets are larger and infrastructures are in place. Furthermore, classical theories pre-dated FAX machines and widespread telecommunications. Doing business abroad is not as prohibitive for small firms with few resources as it was in the past. Therefore, host government incentives or market exchange opportunities may well motivate small firms, young or old, to export or invest abroad.

In summary, classical theories of internationalization assume that businesses will invest abroad in response to changes in supply and demand opportunities. Following the goal of profit maximization, only large firms that have achieved market power or some sort of compensating advantages will be able to consider exploiting international exchange opportunities. Because younger firms are lacking in resources, have informal structures, are concerned with survival, and are generally smaller than established firms, these classical economic theories would presume that new ventures would not have the ability to identify or successfully fulfill international exchange opportunities. Nevertheless, opportunities ignored by large firms may motivate younger small firms to export or invest abroad.

Neoclassical Theories

There are two major neoclassical theories, internalization and diversification. Internalization theories employ transaction cost economics (Williamson, 1978) to explain foreign direct investment, arguing that given cost efficiency as the goal of the firm, the organization will internalize markets to decrease risk (uncertainty) or to safeguard assets (Casson, 1979, pp. 45-65). (See Exhibit #2.1.)

Internalization theories assert that foreign direct investment of multinational enterprises will occur when markets for intangible assets or immediate products are internalized. In order for the MNE to compete with foreign companies in unfamiliar environments, firms need an intangible asset or "ownership advantage" to overcome the disadvantages of doing business abroad (Hymer, 1960; Kindleberger, 1969). MNE's create and possess proprietary assets that they try to exploit internally by extending their organization and control across national boundaries by means of fully owned subsidiaries (Buckley & Casson, 1979; Rugman, 1980). These proprietary assets are referred to as competitive advantages, or firm specific advantages (Hymer, 1960) relative to the firm's competitors (Buckley, 1990) that are based on technology and marketing knowhow (Casson, 1983b; Dunning, 1988). To economize on transaction costs, a company will internalize markets for goods and services through vertical integration, or internalize markets for intangible assets (trade name, know how) through horizontal integration (Caves, 1982). The objective is to seek the least cost location for each activity performed. For example, a company seeking to economize on costs of key supplies may acquire a foreign supplier to lower its transaction costs and achieve greater efficiency. The firm is conceived of as a governance structure and the exchange is the unit of analysis. Hence internalization gives a firm increased control of assets and costs by means of a firm rather than a market solution.

Internalization theories suggest that investment abroad is motivated by attempts to guard specific assets such as information (Casson, 1983b), skills, technology or products, or to gain control over resources (Rugman, 1980; Dunning, 1979) thereby protecting the firm from uncertainty and reducing transaction costs. Implicit in these motives is the rational ability of the firm to assess the costs and benefits of internal or external transaction costs and to implement the decision (Dunning, 1988).

Joint venturing also is a form of foreign market entry for the MNE. These include cooperative arrangements (such as licensing) where control of the MNE is incomplete (less than 100%) (Caves, 1982). The internalization model assumes firms must possess a rent-yielding asset which will allow the company to receive profits and reduce costs in foreign markets. This form of internationalization is frequently used in developing countries and transaction cost logic is applied in explaining motives.

Technology licensing is an alternative form of foreign market entry. This offers a means to overcome foreign market entry barriers (Telesio, 1979) and a different way to gain access to exchange opportunities, or to diversify product/markets (Telesio, 1979). Conditions motivating firms to consider licensing include entry barriers and uncertainty avoidance (Contractor, 1985). In addition, size of the firm, competition, degree of product diversification, and accumulated experience in foreign environments will encourage licensing (Telesio, 1979).

Another explanation for foreign investment arises from theories of international diversification of the MNE. These suggest that a company will multinationalize to spread risk by diversifying into new products/markets (Caves, 1982). Motives for diversification range from industry structure variables (Caves, 1982), to organizational activity within the firm (strategy) (Chandler, 1966). Diversification theories argue that efficiency or risk reduction and profits are goals, and that motives to diversify are based on excess production capacity and possession of a competitive advantage. This theory emphasizes financial aspects of diversification as a means to achieve stability of returns (Buckley & Brooke, 1992).

Taken together, neoclassical theories of internationalization are very useful in explaining foreign direct investment of multinational enterprises. Although these general theories were not intended to discriminate among types of business by size, the assumptions that the goal is cost efficiency and the process of matching transaction costs to governance structures is rational in the choice between internal and external markets, limiting application to large established firms. These assumptions are not consistent with the evidence of the behavior of new ventures. Research has shown that in new companies, goals such as survival (Cooper, Woo & Dunkelberg, 1989; Eggers, Leahy & Churchill, 1994), or high or low growth (Ginn & Sexton, 1990), may dominate, and that the internal decision processes have been found to be intuitive (Miller, 1983) rather than rational and planned (Rice & Hamilton, 1972).

Neoclassical theories also discount the role of management (Casson, 1983, p. 23) by suggesting managers have a simply reactive and evaluative role, often assuming the owner/founder is no longer present (Buckley, 1983, p. 29). In contrast, research in the entrepreneurship field has found the owner/founder to have a dominant and important role in the creation of the strategy of the firm (Cooper, 1981; Stuart & Abetti, 1987; Feeser & Willard, 1990; Shaver & Scott,1991).

For young firms with limited resources and uncertain market acceptance, the choice between internal and external markets as a basis for vertical integration or diversification is not a particularly relevant explanation. Furthermore, newly-formed firms cannot borrow as cheaply as established businesses which limits their ability to internalize markets (Buckley, 1983).

On the other hand, even though these theories discount the role of management as an impetus for the decision to invest abroad, and presume the choice will only be made for cost efficiency reasons, it is possible that possession of a proprietary asset and a desire to spread risk might motivate small firms, young and old. For example, high technology start-ups with patented technology may decide to joint venture or vertically integrate to achieve cost efficiencies in supplies or raw materials.

In sum, neoclassical theories suggest that firms will invest abroad (conceived of as diversification or integration) in order to lower transaction costs. Protection of firm specific advantages or avoidance of market uncertainties are primary motivations in this decision. These theories assume the firm has the resources and internal systems to compare and contrast internal versus external transaction costs, and only seem to explain the international business activities of large established businesses. However, motives such as possession of a competitive advantage or desire to achieve cost efficiencies may motivate small firms to joint venture or invest abroad. Neoclassical theories do not seem to apply to new firms that possess limited resources, are under dominant owner/-manager control, and face a higher cost of capital.

THEORIES OF ENTREPRENEURSHIP

Theories of entrepreneurship have their roots in four disciplines; economics, business history/anthropology, psychology, and sociology. Major dimensions of entrepreneurship identified from these streams are risk-bearing, creation, innovation and general management activities (Sandberg, 1992). (See Exhibit #2.1.) These theories do not specifically address reasons why new ventures will internationalize, but they do provide relevant information about dimensions of venture creation, start-up strategies and how new ventures will approach market opportunities. Following is a discussion of how these theories may help explaining internationalization considered from each disciplinary perspective.

The economics perspective conceives of new venture creation as a new innovation or carrying out of "new combinations" and where growth occurs by creating new demand (or new markets) (Schumpeter, 1942). This is characterized as reforming or revolutionizing production patterns, developing new technologies, new sources or new commodities (Schumpeter, 1942). The key focus is the "innovation" and its role in destabilization of pre-existing economic systems. It is proposed that new business firms will be created when an individual envisions an invention, acquires the resources to develop it, creates the enterprise, and grows it successfully (Kirchoff (1991) on Schumpeter [1942]). The invention, a new combination of ideas, is implemented when entrepreneurs enter existing markets by creating new firms, resulting in disequilibrium. If successful, new firms "destroy" the structure of oligopolistic markets, thereby creating new wealth (Schumpeter, 1942). Relatedly, scholars have defined the "entrepreneur" as the person who notices a profit-making opportunity that others have overlooked (Kirzner, 1982), or perceives "gaps" in markets then acts to connect or fill them (Liebenstein, 1968). The notion of financial risk often is associated with economics theories (Knight, 1921).

The business history/anthropology tradition conceives of new venture creation as a purposeful activity to create a profitable enterprise (Cole, 1965). The process is socio-cultural and it is the role of the venture creator, his/her life, career, and decision process, that provides the basis for theories (Stewart, 1991). These theories focus on actions and activities involved in seizing opportunities, which are a function of accumulation of knowledge, skills and resources (Stewart, 1991). Business history, often referred to as "tycoon history", emphasizes the role of the general manager in controlling and allocating capital (Chandler, 1964). It is the social and cultural factors that determine the skills and resources available to the creator pursuing the opportunity.

Alternatively, work by David McClelland (1961) in the psychology area proposes that new venture creation is a function of the qualities of individuals, in particular those who possess a high need for achievement. McClelland argued that it is the individual's psychological characteristics, such as need for achievement, risk-taking propensity and locus of control, that explain why and how new ventures will be born. Empirical work did not support this. Brockhaus (1980) found that there were few differences in risk propensity between entrepreneurs and managers. In recent years, trait theories have become less popular as explanations for entrepreneurial behavior. On the other hand, cognitive theories recently have gained credibility (Shaver & Scott, 1991). These theories suggest it is cognitive factors such as perceptions, beliefs, and conceptions of opportunities in a social context that influences venture creation (Bird, 1992; Katz, 1992). Recognizing the importance of economic circumstances, social networks, teams, marketing, finance, and public agency support, the cognitive perspective argues that the most critical and necessary element is "...a person, in whose mind all of the possibilities come together, who believes that the innovation is possible, and who has the motivation to persist until the job is done" (Shaver & Scott, 1991, p.39).

The sociology perspective asserts that social systems and their actors will influence creation of productive organizations (Reynolds, 1991). Two alternative models are proposed. One is an equilibrium model evolving from Parsons and Smelser (1956), and the other is rooted in Karl Marx's ideas of class conflict (Reynolds, 1991). These theories note that societies provide the opportunities that new venture creators may take advantage of. Further, it is the features of a person's social context that affect his/her perception of these opportunities and the decision to seize them. In other words, status in society as an elite or socially marginal individual can impact ability and propensity to be entrepreneurial, create or produce a new situation (Hoselitz, 1963). These features are life course stage, context in social networks, ethnic identification, and organizational/population industry life course stage (Reynolds, 1991). It is society that determines the "windows of opportunity" for groups of individuals. A broader view combines personal and social dimensions into a push-pull framework, where the "creation event" is the definition of entrepreneurship (Shapero & Sokol, 1982).

While each of these theories of entrepreneurship offer credible explanations for the creation of new enterprises, none of these theories alone adequately explains why new ventures internationalize. These theories suggest causes and process of new venture creation but do not explicitly address the choice of internationalization as a characteristic, condition or action at start-up. Furthermore, from this discussion it is apparent there is no single unified theory of entrepreneurship and the phenomenon is complex and multi-dimensional (Gartner, 1985). Each of these four disciplines provide dimensions important to the characteristics of new venture creation, which can be summarized as business activity composed of some combination of the following:

a. *innovation*—the commercial exploitation of some new products, process, market, materials or organization (Schumpeter, 1942)

b. *general management* —the managerial direction of, or resource allocation for business units as a whole (Cole, 1965; Stevenson & Gumpert, 1984; McClelland, 1961; Chandler, 1964; Sandberg, 1992)

c. *risk-bearing*—acceptance of risk from the potential losses or failure of a business unit (Palmer, 1971; McClelland, 1961; Knight, 1921)

d. *creation*— reation of a new organization to pursue opportunity (Katz & Gartner, 1988; Gartner, 1985; Timmons 1985; Vesper, 1990, Bygrave & Hofer, 1991)

While not intended to explain internationalization, these entrepreneurial dimensions are generally present in the creation of new ventures. Because internationalized small companies are arguably entrepreneurial, in that they are perceiving new opportunities, assuming some risk and creating value, consideration of dimensions from entrepreneurship may explain the motivation of young businesses to sell products abroad. (Sandberg, 1992). For example; the *innovation* (product, its characteristics and distinct advantages), and market characteristics (growth, size and competition) might be a reason for selecting an international market. On the other hand, *general management* factors such as founders' cultural background (language, country/community of origin) and experiences (course of study, type of occupational experiences) might be important in the creator's perception and implementation of international opportunities. Likewise, the willingness of the management team to seek or accept *risk*, in particular financial risk, with regards to international opportunities or domestic threats may motivate international expansion. Finally, factors important to *creation*, such as the background of founders (level of education, years of occupational experience, age, social status, ethnicity), resources (supply of labor, information, capital or physical facilities) or environmental conditions (economic trends, competition) might influence a new venture creator's propensity to seek opportunities in international markets as part of a venture's start-up strategy.

In sum, even though theories of entrepreneurship were not intended to explain international expansion, dimensions of these theories— innovation, general management, risk-bearing, and creation—may shed light on the causes of internationalization by young businesses.

TOWARD A NEW THEORETICAL MODEL

Both the classical and neoclassical theories from the industrial economics stream of international business literature presume that a business has a substantive history and size. Therefore, explanations for foreign direct investment and exporting are based on assumptions that the firm's goal is profit maximization or cost efficiency, the organizational structure is hierarchical in nature, and a market position has been established, and the owner/founder has a minor role. Firm and industry factors are the major motivators in the decision to internationalize.

Behavioral theories suggest that companies will export or invest abroad when they face some type of environmental threat or opportunity. The internationalization process is an alternative for responding to these threats or opportunities, and it is achieved in an incremental stepwise fashion. Perceptions of environmental conditions are major factors in the decision to internationalize. It is assumed that the business has experience and the capability to implement such a decision.

Theories from entrepreneurship rooted in economics, business history/anthropology, psychology and sociology are useful for explaining factors important in new venture creation process. These theories suggest that individual characteristics (background, experiences, and cognition), organizational aspects (resources and product/service characteristics), and socio-cultural and market factors are important in the start-up of new ventures. None of these entrepreneurial theories alone will explain why a young venture will internationalize, nor do they specifically address why a small business would sell its products abroad. However, considered together their theories suggest factors that might explain the international dimensions of a new venture strategy.

There have been recent efforts to create a theory of "global start-ups", (McDougall, Oviatt & Brush, 1991; Ray, 1991), defined as "international new ventures that from inception engage in international business" (McDougall, 1989, p. 388). This work is based on a grounded theory approach to examining the phenomenon of new ventures that were internationalized at start-up. Global start-ups are conceived of as new businesses that are born international. Their location, sources of suppliers and resources, buyers, and distribution channels are in multiple countries. Oviatt & McDougall,(1994) have proposed that resource availability, global vision of the creator, and some sort of competitive advantage are important to this process.

In order to better explain the motivations for small businesses, both young and old to internationalize, a synthesis of theories is needed. As McDougall, Shane & Oviatt (1994) have argued, international business theories are limited in explaining behavior of international new ventures. Exhibit #2.2 reflects a summary of theoretical dimensions from international business and entrepreneurship. Taken together, aspects from these theories may explain reasons why small businesses, either young or old, decide to internationalize. This combination of theoretical factors includes four distinct levels of analysis: managerial, firm, industry, and environment. By considering all four of these dimensions, a more complete explanation of motivations is possible. Furthermore, possible motives for internationalization from all the theories discussed herein is presented in Exhibit #2.3.

SUMMARY

In summary, theories of international business identify factors that explain why businesses (big or small) will internationalize. Together these theories assume businesses have experience—they are established in the marketplace, possess sufficient resources and capabilities, are frequently large in size, will follow a logical stepwise progression in increasing commitment and risk, and are attempting to avoid uncertainty. Because young ventures lack experience, are resource constrained, have

Exhibit #2.2

INTEGRATED SUMMARY OF THEORETICAL FACTORS CONTRIBUTING
TO THE DECISION TO INTERNATIONALIZE

	INTERNATIONAL BUSINESS			ENTREPRENEURSHIP
	Behavioral	*Classical*	*Neoclassical*	
	Exporting, Foreign Investment	Direct Investment	Horizontal and Vertical Integration	New Venture Creation
Management Factors	Perceptions of threats/ opportunities Expectations Skills	-------	-------	Cultural/ethnic background Education and occupational experiences Demographics Vision
Firm Factors	Experience Resources Organ- izational learning	Firm advantage Size Market position	Firm advantage Specific assets information, skills technology, product, resources	Product characteristics Resources Innovation
Industry Factors	-------	Industry structure; concentration, maturity, size	Competition	Characteristics; growth, size Market conditions
Environ- mental Factors	Market, socio- cultural, demographic, political, opport- unities/ threats	Exchange opportunities domestically/abroad	Uncertain market conditions	Opportunity to innovate

Exhibit #2.3

SUMMARY OF MOTIVATIONS TO INTERNATIONALIZE FROM THEORIES OF INTERNATIONAL BUSINESS AND ENTREPRENEURSHIP

	Behavioral	*Classical*	*Neoclassical*	*Entrepreneurship*
	Export; FDI	FDI; International Diversification	Horizontal/Vertical Integration	New Venture Creation
Motives				
Resolve problem, avoid risk	+	+	+	*
Pursue opportunity	+			*
Executive push	+			*
Profit	+	+		*
Political imperative		+		*
Industry structure		+		*
Economize on costs		+	+	*
Competitive advantage		+	+	*
Spread risk		+		*
Innovation				#
Creation				#
Risk-bearing				#
General management				#

+- Motives for direct investment or exporting as noted from theories of international business
*- Motives stated from theories of international business that may be associated with the decision of small young and old businesses.
#- Factors in the decision to create new ventures

not achieved market position, frequently do not avoid risk, do not plan formally and the owner/founder plays a dominant role, these theories do not seem to apply in this context. However, many of the variables from these theories have not been tested in the context of small business, and it is quite possible that some of these variables from the international business domain may motivate both young and old small businesses to export or invest abroad.

On the other hand, theories from entrepreneurship are useful for explaining motivations for the start-up of a new venture. These theories, with roots in economics, business history/anthropology, psychology and sociology, suggest various factors that are important to the start-up strategy of a new venture. But, they do not explicitly address reasons for internationalization or suggest how internationalization might occur in established small businesses. Four major dimensions identified from entrepreneurship theories—risk bearing, innovation, creation, and general management,— may affect the decision to internationalize because small businesses, and in particular new internationalized businesses are arguably entrepreneurial.

Taken together, dimensions from theories of both international business and entrepreneurship offer reasons for the internationalization of small businesses of any age. While these theories are helpful, it is important to consider the empirical tests of these variables. The following chapter reviews the empirical literature from international business related to motives for small business internationalization.

III

Empirical Literature Review

The majority of studies on international activities of small businesses have been conducted in the field of International Marketing. These studies investigate motives for exporting, differences between exporters and non-exporters, and factors leading to export success. Research in International Business is abundant on foreign direct investment and licensing in large multi-nationals, but there are few studies of small companies. Most recently, studies have emerged in the Entrepreneurship field that examine globalization and international strategies of new companies. As background to the investigation described in this book, 83 studies were reviewed, from which variables encouraging internationalization were identified.

MOTIVES FOR INTERNATIONALIZATION

Empirical studies of factors motivating businesses to invest abroad or export employ a range of theories. Because the purpose of this investigation is not to establish the validity of any particular theory from any single field, but to identify which variables from different theories that will shed light on the motives for internationalization by small businesses, this chapter reviews studies from international marketing, international economics, international diversification, internalization, entrepreneurship, political economy, international business and business strategy. It is important to note that each of these areas define international business activities differently. For example, studies from international marketing consider internationalization to be operationalized as exporting, whereas international diversification and international economics are mainly concerned with foreign direct investment. In order to cover studies about international business activities of small companies, this review defines internationalization broadly to include direct investment, licensing, and exporting. Studies about importing are beyond the scope of this review and will not be considered. While this review is not comprehensive, it covers 83 studies and is representative of the body of empirical work investigating factors motivating small businesses to internationalize. Appendix A includes a complete listing of studies covered in this review by author, date, purpose, sample and findings.

As noted above, the bulk of research on international activities of small companies is found in field of International Marketing. Most of this research concentrates on the propensity of small firms to export (Ursic & Czinkota, 1984; Cavusgil, 1984; O'Rourke, 1985; Pak & Weaver, 1990; Holzmuller & Kasper, 1990); differences between exporters and non-exporters (Tookey, 1964; Langston & Teas, 1976; Bilkey, 1978; Weidersheim-Paul, et al, 1978; Whithey, 1980; Kedia & Chokar, 1985; Johnston & Czinkota, 1982); and factors leading to export success (Tookey, 1964; Sweeney, 1970; Johnston & Czinkota, 1982; Cooper & Kleinschmidt, 1985; Christensen, et al, 1987; Holzmuller & Kasper, 1990; Bijmolt & Zwart, 1994; Dominguez & Sequeira, 1993; Kaynak, 1992; Liouville, 1992).

The majority of these studies on propensity to export, differences between exporters and non-exporters, and factors leading to export success have concentrated on managers' characteristics as motives. For example, topics of major investigation include the manager's background (skills, travel experience, education), his/her attitude toward international business, and his/her perceptions of risks, and costs or opportunities in international expansion. This focus is explainable because in the research that is theory based, Aharoni's (1966) and Johanson and Vahlne's (1977) behavioral explanations of the management decision process serve as a foundation for the empirical research (Reid, 1980; Ursic & Czinkota, 1984; Welch & Weidersheim-Paul, 1980; Holzmuller & Kasper, 1990, 1991).

While most theory and many empirical studies presume that the decision to internationalize is intentional and planned, several studies show the opposite to be true. Companies frequently sell products abroad in response to "unsolicited orders" (Bilkey, 1978; Beamish & Munro, 1986; Kaynak, 1992). One study explored differences between passive and reactive exporters (Piercy, 1981) finding distinctions in size, product and volume. Relatedly, Eramilli & Rao (1990) found differences in small service exporters in that "client followers" and "market seekers" differed in level of export involvement.

Collectively, these studies from International Marketing suggest that in small companies a positive attitude of the owner/founder will distinguish between exporters and non-exporters and influence success. Similarly, perceptions of costs, risks, and opportunities also will differentiate between exporters and non-exporters.

Studies from international business investigating motives for other forms of internationalization (foreign direct investment, licensing, and joint venturing) have employed theories from industrial economics, political economy and internalization. The majority of these studies investigate activities of the multinational enterprise, and many are applications of economic models to existing data bases (see, for example, Kobrin, 1991; Telesio, 1979; Chatterjee, 1990). Few researchers have investigated the decision to license or invest abroad in small firms, although more recent work includes Kohn's (1988) investigation of small firms foreign direct investment activities; LeCraw's (1989) research on small firm counter-trade; Galbraith, et al's (1990) research on U.S. firms locating to Mexico; and Tyebjee's (1990) work on high technology licensing activities of new ventures.

Lorange and Roos (1990) recently studied differences in formation of cooperative ventures in Norway and Sweden, finding distinct differences in goals and analytical approach. For companies in both countries, entrepreneurial management factors were significant in the decision.

This work on foreign direct investment and licensing of small firms suggests that firm factors, such as competitive advantage (LeCraw, 1989), technological advantage (Gomes-Casseres & Kohn, 1990), and environmental conditions (Galbraith, et al, 1990) are important in the decision to internationalize. Of the studies on larger companies, many firm, industry and environmental variables have been found to be important in the decision to invest abroad. These include the existence of a competitive advantage, scale economies, low entry barriers, and low political risk. (See Caves, 1982 for further discussion of these factors.)

Recent case study work on forces driving the creation of "global start-ups" (Oviatt, McDougall & Dinterman, 1993) found resources, markets and internal factors contributed to formation. Further, this work also identified seven keys to success, which were global vision, management with international experience, international networks, technology advantage, unique assets, linked product/service extension, and tight organizational coordination.

FIRM CHARACTERISTICS AND
INTERNATIONAL STRATEGIES

Firm characteristics are important in the decision to sell products abroad. Many studies have investigated the effect of firm size in the decision to export and in exporting success. The results are inconclusive (Miesenbock, 1988) largely because size has been operationalized many different ways making it difficult for researchers to compare results across studies (Reid,1980). Operationalizations vary from sales break-downs (Cavusgil, 1984), to employee categories (Bilkey & Tesar, 1977). The term "small" can range from less than $1,000,000 (Johnston & Czinkota, 1982) to less than $20,000,000 in sales (Abdel Malek, 1978; Cavusgil, 1984), or from less than 100 employees (Bilkey & Tesar, 1977) to less than 1000 employees (Kohn, 1988).[5] Despite difficulties in generalizing across studies, some trends are evident.Some studies have found that size doesn't matter in the decision to export (Abdel Malek, 1978; Walters & Saimee, 1990), and doesn't limit ability or affect export intensity (Calof, 1993). Several more studies have found that large size is important (Christensen, et al, 1987; O'Rourke, 1985; Gripsrud, 1989; Tyebjee, 1990). There is less evidence that size is related to export success (Cooper & Kleinschmidt, 1985; Calof, 1993), but results show size does affect international strategy in terms of geographic scope of operations (Gripsrud, 1989; Cavusgil & Naor, 1987) and quality control (Christensen, et al, 1987). Recently Calof (1993) found in a large Canadian study that large companies were more likely to be profitable, however Loiuville (1992) found size was not significantly related to profitability in a study of West German engineering firms.

Exploration of international strategy in small businesses has been investigated in recent studies where product characteristics (McDougall, 1989; Gripsrud, 1989) and market research (Sriram & Sapienza, 1990), and business planning (Bijmolt & Zwart, 1994) have been found important in affecting type of international strategy pursued. Baird, Lyles & Orris (1994) investigated small companies' choice of international strategy finding larger manufacturers were more likely to be international-ized and practice formal planning than non-internationalized companies. Planning also has been studied (Walters, 1993) and findings showed that contrary to normative literature, planning was not related to growth except in very small companies. In general, research on international strategies of small businesses is a relatively new area of investigation.

Another area where results are inconclusive is the effect of firm age in the decision to internationalize. Company age has been researched in a few studies as it relates to differences between exporters and non-exporters in the decision to sell products abroad. Kirplani and McIntosh (1981), Ursic and Czinkota (1984), and Pinney (1970) found that younger firms were more likely to export, whereas Welch and Weidersheim-Paul (1980) concluded that older firms were more likely to export. Pak and Weaver (1990) concluded age didn't matter. However, none of these studies investigated the effect of age on the decision. Furthermore, none of these studies have considered the entrepreneurial characteristics of young firms and the role these might play in such a decision, instead assuming few differences between new and established small businesses.

In general, studies from international marketing are in many cases applied rather than theory driven. As a result, many of these are descriptive in nature, cross sectional by design and frequently consider only individual characteristics and perceptions as the independent variable related to the decision to export (see Appendix A for further description of studies).

FACTORS AFFECTING INTERNATIONALIZATION

Collectively, these studies suggest that variables motivating internationalization can be grouped across levels. (See Exhibit #3.1.) Categories of factors influencing the decision to internationalize include management, the firm, and industry variables. Perceived favorability/unfavorability of domestic and host country environments also have been found significant. Research shows that many characteristics of the owner/founder contribute to the decision to internationalize (Bilkey, 1978; Reid, 1980). Specifically, work and travel experiences abroad (Bilkey, 1978; Johanson & Vahlne, 1978), higher level of education (Simpson & Kujawa, 1974), skills in finance and planning (Cavusgil & Naor, 1987), and personal contacts for information sources (Cavusgil & Naor, 1987). Besides these characteristics, a favorable attitude of management towards internationalization also contributed to the decision to go international (Reid, 1980; Kedia & Chokar, 1985; Lindquist, 1990; Holzmuller & Kasper, 1991).

Firm level factors also are relevant to a small business' decision to invest abroad or export. These include the age, size, resources, firm advantage and life cycle of the company. There is conflicting evidence about effects of size (Cavusgil & Naor, 1987); and age has only been

Exhibit #3.1

VARIABLES CONTRIBUTING TO DECISION TO INTERNATIONALIZE

Management Variables

experience	Bilkey, 1978; Ali & Swiercz, 1991; Cavusgil, 1982; Gripsrud, 1989; Cavusgil & Naor, 1987; Pak & Weaver, 1990
education level (high)	Simpson & Kujawa, 1974; Cavusgil & Naor, 1987
lived/worked abroad	Bilkey, 1978; Langston & Teas, 1976
speaks foreign language	Bilkey, 1978
favorable attitude toward internationalization	Reid, 1980; Cooper & Kleinschmidt, 1985; Kedia & Chokar, 1985; Sriram & Sapienza; 1991; Lindquist, 1990; Weidersheim-Paul,et al 1978; Ursic & Czinkota, 1984; Gripsrud, 1989; Pinney, 1970; Holzmuller & Kasper, 1990; 1991; Cavusgil, 1979; Withey, 1980
business skills	Cavusgil & Naor, 1987
information contacts	O'Rourke, 1985; Cavusgil & Naor, 1987
perceptions of risk/ opportunities	Aharoni, 1966; Roy & Simpson, 1981; Simpson & Kujawa, 1974; Kwei Chong & Wai Chong, 1988; Bilkey, 1978; Kedia & Chokar, 1985; Rabino, 1980; Sullivan & Bauerschmidt, 1990; Cavusgil & Nevin, 1984; Galbraith, et al, 1990; Kaynak, 1992
commitment to expansion and growth	Cavusgil, 1982; 1984; Cavusgil & Nevin, 1981; Sweeney, 1970; Lindquist, 1990; Lorange & Roos, 1990; Aaby & Slater, 1989; Singer & Czinkota; 1992

Firm Variables

old age   Snavely, et al, 1964; Welch &
                            Weidersheim-Paul, 1980

young age   Ursic & Czinkota, 1984; Pinney, 1970
                            Kirplani & McIntosh, 1980; Oviatt,
                            McDougall & Dintermann, 1993

life cycle stage   Cavusgil, 1984

resources-
  management time   Simpson & Kujawa, 1974

  capital   Bilkey, 1978; Chatterjee, 1990;
                            Tyebjee,1990; Reid, 1980; Lindquist, 1990;
                            Simpson & Kujawa, 1974

  skilled personnel   Rourke, 1985; Tesar, 1977

  information   Reid, 1984; Cavusgil & Naor, 1987
                            Bilkey, 1978

  large size   Tookey, 1964; LeCraw, 1983; Horst,
                            1972; Withey, 1980; Telesio,
                            1979; Gripsrud, 1989; O'Rourke,
                            1985; Christensen, et al, 1987;
                            Hirsch & Adar, 1974; Roy & Simpson,
                            1981; Bijmolt & Zwart, 1994; Baird,
                            Lyles & Orris, 1994

  experience   Telesio, 1979; LeCraw, 1989
  internationally

Firm Variables (continued)

specific advantage -   Hymer, 1960; Kothari, 1978; LeCraw,
                         1983; Welch & Weidersheim -Paul, 1980
                         Aaby & Slater, 1989; Bijmolt & Zwart,
                         1994

technology   Gomes-Casseres & Kohn, 1990; Tesar,
                         1977; Robock & Simmonds, 1983; Johnston
                         & Czinkota, 1982; Kohn, 1988; McDougall,
                         1989

product   Namiki, 1988; Gripsrud, 1989; Cavusgil,
characteristics   1982; McDougall, 1989; Robock &
                         Simmonds, 1983; LeCraw, 1989; Ursic &
                         Czinkota, 1984; Cavusgil & Naor, 1987;
                         Aaby & Slater, 1989; Baird, Lyles & Orris,
                         1994

economies of scale   Caves, 1982; Buckley, 1983; Kobrin, 1991

cost advantage   Kohn, 1988; Vernon, 1971

control of resources   Rugman, 1979; Dunning, 1980

access to distribution   Tesar, 1977; Cavusgil & Naor,
channels   1987; Malezadeh & Nahavandi, 1985

Industry Variables

type   Buckley & Casson, 1979

competition   Telesio, 1979; Kothari, 1978; Adams
                         & Hall, 1993

structure   Dunning, 1979; Contractor, 1985

Environmental Variables

opportunities	Aharoni, 1966
market opportunities demand/potential	Hymer, 1960; Cooper & Kleinschmidt, 1985 Clegg, 1990; Green & Cunningham, 1975; Kohn, 1988; D'Souza & Eramilli, 1990; Holzmuller, & Kasper, 1990
resources information	Galbraith, et al 1990 Goodnow & Hansz, 1972; Bilkey, 1978; Cavusgil & Nevin, 1981
positive government, geo-cultural political, legal, physiographic environment	Goodnow & Hansz, 1972; Galbraith, et al, 1990; Clegg, 1990; Malezadeh & Nahavandi, 1985; Hisrich & Peters, 1983
unsolicited orders	Bilkey & Tesar, 1977; O'Rourke, 1985; Simpson & Kujawa, 1974; Welch & Weidersheim-Paul, 1980; Beamish & Munro; 1986; Kaynak, 1992 D'Souza & Eramilli,1990
geographic closeness	Galbraith, et al, 1990; Tesar, 1977; Malezadeh & Nahavandi, 1985
cultural closeness	Welch & Weidersheim-Paul, 1980; Sullivan & Bauerschmidt, 1990

investigated as a descriptive variable. For instance, Ursic & Czinkota (1984) found younger firms more likely to export while Welch & Wiedersheim-Paul(1980) found older firms more likely to export. Relatedly the life cycle stage of the business has been found to motivate the decision of small businesses to internationalize (Cavusgil, 1984), where firms in later stages are more likely to export than businesses in early stages. Resources are similarly important; capital (Tyebjee, 1990), skilled personnel (O'Rourke,1985), and information (1980) all have been found to be important variables.

Firm-specific advantage also has been associated with likelihood of exporting in several studies. These include marketing skills, technologies and products (Robock & Simmonds, 1983), and unique relations with customers (Marchesnay & Julien, 1990). Various aspects of product characteristics such as patents (Baird, Lyles & Orris, 1994) development capability and uniqueness (Cavusgil, 1982) and technology (Kohn, 1988) have been found to influence the decision to internationalize.

Industry factors important to the decision to invest abroad are type of industry (Buckley and Casson, 1979), industry structure (Dunning, 1979), and competitive conditions (Welch & Weidersheim-Paul, 1980). Intense competition that limits domestic opportunity (Kothari, 1978), or size of competitors (Adams & Hall, 1993) also have encouraged internationalization.

Environmental conditions (resources, economic, technological, and legal aspects) both in the U.S. (Galbraith, et al, 1990; Kaynak, 1992) and in the host country (Kohn, 1988; Malezadeh & Nahavandi, 1985; Hisrich & Peters, 1983; Adams & Hall, 1993), have been noted as motivators to export or invest abroad. Aspects such as cultural closeness of the foreign market (Welch & Weidersheim-Paul, 1980) and geographic distance have also been noted (Malezadeh & Nahavandi, 1985). As noted earlier, several studies have noted that one of the prime motives for exporting is the receipt of unsolicited orders from abroad (Bilkey & Tesar, 1977; Simpson & Kujawa, 1974; Beamish & Munro, 1986; D'Souza & Eramilli, 1990; Kaynak, 1992).

SUMMARY

Extensive research on small business internationalization exists in the field of International Marketing where managerial perceptions and characteristics as determinants in the decision to export have been widely studies. Differences between exporting and non-exporting businesses (the most popular form of international activity for small business [Miesenbock, 1988]) are well researched, however less work has considered other forms of international activity such as licensing or joint venturing. Research in other areas of international business concentrates on foreign direct investment by large businesses, but a few recent studies about small firms show industry factors, competitive advantage, and environmental factors are important. In all, the predominant empirical research on small company internationalization has focused on established companies, or failed to consider possible variations resultant from organizational age. As noted earlier in Chapter II, there are significant differences between new and established small companies. It is reasonable to believe these differences will be in evidence when considering factors motivating internationalization.

NOTES

1. The most common operationalization of size is number of employees, and consistent with the SBA and Department of Commerce, a small business is one with less than 500 employees (Roy & Simpson, 1981; Withey, 1980).

IV
Methodology and Research Design

OVERVIEW

This research investigates reasons why small businesses decide to internationalize and compares motives based on age of company at internationalization. Company age has not been previously investigated as a factor in internationalization. Furthermore it is assumed that small new companies won't be able or desire to sell products abroad until after they have gained market experience. A variety of motives are proposed by different theories. For exporting, it is argued management decision-making factors motivate businesses to sell abroad, whereas for foreign direct investment, company advantages, industry structures, and/or environmental conditions affect the decision. Theories of foreign direct investment ignore the role of the manager which is prominent in small companies, whereas management decision-making explanations place little importance on structural or environmental factors. On the other hand, theories of entrepreneurship emphasize the role and vision of the owner/founder in new venture start-up strategies. In sum, no single theory appears to explain small business investment abroad or exporting.

Because no single theory from international business or entrepreneurship fully explains why young and old small businesses will internationalize, it makes sense to combine key elements of these theories to test the research questions that guide this study. This is similar to Merton's (1962) mid-range theory which is designed to guide empirical inquiry intermediate to general theory and appropriate for specific classes of social behavior. Given the exploratory nature of this study, a broad framework was developed that combined four levels of variables (management, firm, industry, and environment) derived from neoclassical, classical and behavioral theories of international business, and

47

theories of entrepreneurship. Other researchers in international business have used this approach (Chatterjee, 1990; Geringer, et al, 1989).

Empirical research on multinational enterprises has concentrated on identification of company and industry structural variables motivating foreign direct investment of large businesses, most of which are old. Research in international marketing has focused on management variables and perceptions of the environment to explain differences between exporting and non-exporting small businesses. The limited research in entrepreneurship related to international activities has concentrated on characteristics of international entrepreneurs, differences between exporters and non-exporters in motivations to internationalize, and international strategies (Namiki, 1988; McDougall, 1989). Research to date has ignored characteristics and differences in small companies that emerge due to age. These acknowledged distinctions may similarly explain behavior of companies internationalizing from start up, as well as disentangle conflicting results from studies about size. Four broad questions guide this research:

1. What factors motivate young small businesses to engage in international business activities?

2. What factors motivate old small businesses to engage in international business activities?

3. Do reasons for internationalization vary significantly by age of small business?

4. Do international strategies vary by age of small business?

The next section proposes a conceptual framework and develops hypotheses for exploring these questions.

CONCEPTUAL FRAMEWORK AND VARIABLES

The framework guiding this research was developed from a synthesis of empirical and theoretical literature from international business and entrepreneurship. There are five main constructs; Contextual Factors, Strategy, Performance, Regional Environment Conditions and Host Country Conditions (See Exhibit #4.1). *Contextual Factors* are composed of management, firm and industry elements, and they are critically important to determining patterns of strategy variables for a business (Morrison & Roth, 1989, p. 42; Buckley & Casson, 1978,p. 7). *International Strategy* is composed of exchange activities whereby the business uses resources and skills to differentiate products/services to serve both U.S. and international customers (Morrison & Roth, 1989, p. 30). These activities include the decision to internationalize, a mode of foreign market entry (export, licensing or contracting, or foreign direct investment) (Buckley, 1989; Akther & Friedman, 1989), and degree of internationalization (geographic scope [Thorelli, 1987; McDougall, 1989] and commitment [Cavusgil, 1984] to international activities).

The result of these behaviors is some type of business performance. *Performance* is an outcome variable descriptive of an organization's progress toward its goals or activities relative to competitors. Performance of an internationalized firm is frequently measured in financial terms (D'Souza & Eramilli, 1991; Geringer, Beamish, daCosta, 1989) where sales growth and profits from domestic, foreign, and overall operations are considered.

Influencing these three constructs are two sets of environmental conditions: regional environment conditions and host country conditions. *Regional Environment Conditions* include local economic, political-regulatory and demographic factors (Buckely & Casson, 1978, p. 7). These are perceptions of the immediate environment domestically (in this research, U.S.) as it affects the business. *Host Country Conditions* are composed of economic, political-legal and cultural (Goodnow & Hansz, 1972; Mascarenhas, 1982) opportunities and risks.

The relationships explored in this study are indicated by solid lines on Exhibit #4.1. The main constructs of interest are contextual factors, regional environment conditions, host country factors, and international aspects of strategy. Contextual factors are the independent variables, and international strategy (foreign market entry mode and degree of internationalization—geographic scope and committee) are the dependent variables. The deliberate narrowing of this project to these aspects does not suggest performance is not an important element. To the contrary, performance is important when predicting the successful entry and effectiveness of international strategy over time, and it is highly related to the other two constructs. Furthermore, it is important to understand the antecedents to internationalization before examining performance outcomes. However, inclusion of this dimension would significantly

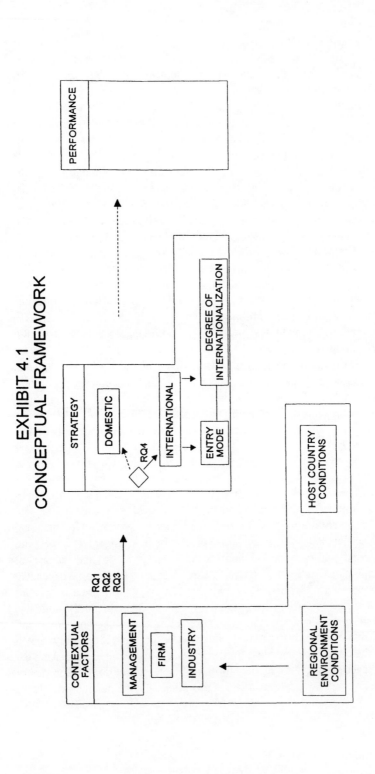

EXHIBIT 4.1
CONCEPTUAL FRAMEWORK

increase the scope of this project and require longitudinal measures. Therefore, descriptive performance information was collected, and questions relating to the impact of international strategy on performance will be investigated at a future time.

Furthermore, an investigation of the cognitive processes involved in the decision to internationalize also is beyond the scope of this study. While an understanding of how owner/managers gain information, evaluate, interpret and act on international opportunities is important to our knowledge of the behavior of young and old small businesses, exploratory investigation to identify the general categories of factors related to the decision is a necessary preliminary step.

Similarly, extensive understanding of the regional environment and host country conditions as they affect international strategy are very important. However, inclusion of comprehensive measures of economic, political-legal and cultural conditions in several host countries, in addition to acquiring measures of economic, political-regulatory and demographic conditions across the U.S., was not possible for this research. Therefore, perceptual measures and secondary data was collected for these two constructs to provide some perspective on external aspects affecting the decision to engage in international business.

Finally, the domestic and overall strategies of a small business are integrally related to its international strategy. The similarities, differences, and relationships between these strategies are questions worthy of investigation but will be pursued in a future research project.

HYPOTHESES

This study investigates factors motivating internationalization of small businesses. Theories of international business offer reasons why established small businesses will export or invest abroad, and theories of entrepreneurship explain how new ventures are created and develop start-up strategies. Research questions were developed to explore the reasons for internationalization in small businesses considering the effect of business age at the time of the decision. This book argues that no single theory fully explains motivations of small businesses to internationalize, therefore consistent with these research questions, hypotheses were developed to test application of theoretical constructs from the fields of entrepreneurship and international business.

Hypotheses provide a link between empirical findings and theory predictions about values of units of a theory in which empirical indicators are employed for the named units in each proposition (Dubin, 1978). Given the purpose of this study is to describe factors and analyze their association with each other rather than to predict, the hypotheses are analytical rather than predictive (Sekaran, 1984), requiring that these hypotheses focus on differences between groups and relationships and associations of factors to these groups. The major questions addressed in this research deal with differences in motivations of small businesses at the time of internationalization and any possible differences, therefore the hypotheses address aspects of small business behavior that might be expected to differ by age. Four sets of hypotheses are proposed relative to the research questions stated earlier in this discussion and are summarized in Exhibit #4.2.

Research Question #1. What factors motivate young small businesses to engage in international business activities?

Theoretical and empirical research from entrepreneurship notes that the role of the manager is prominent in young small businesses (Cooper, 1981; Churchill & Lewis, 1983). For example, the start-up strategy of a young company is highly related to the personal background and experiences of the owner-founder. Typically, young ventures lack resources (Cooper & Dunkelberg, 1986) and are characterized by an undefined organizational structure, informal procedures, and flexible policies (Churchill & Lewis, 1983). Due to their age, these businesses lack market experience and are often in the process of refining product characteristics and strategies, relying strongly on the vision of the owner/founder (Cooper, 1981; Bird, 1989). Given the dominant role of the manager in young ventures and consistent with theories from entrepreneurship, it is expected that management variables will be the most frequently mentioned by young businesses as reasons for internationalizing.

> *Hyp. #1*—In young small businesses, management factors will provide greater explanation for their reasons to internationalize than will firm, industry, regional environment, or host country factors.

Research Question #2. What factors motivate old small businesses to engage in international business activities?

Old small businesses are characterized by established patterns of decision-making (Churchill & Lewis, 1983), experienced employees (Cooper, 1981) and identifiable administrative structures (Churchill & Lewis, 1983). By virtue of their age, these businesses have a track record of experience and product performance on which to base strategic decisions. Systems and planning more frequently occur and growth or expansion are typical goals (Churchill & Lewis, 1983; Lippit & Schmidt, 1967; Eggers, Leahy & Churchill, 1994). The benefit of experience and organized procedures provides knowledge and information about industry conditions, and their track record of operations establishes their position in an industry. Given the importance of the characteristics of older small businesses, and consistent with theories from international business that assume experience, resources and capabilities will drive internationalization, it is expected that firm variables will be the most often mentioned by these businesses as reasons for selling abroad.

Hyp.# 2—In old small businesses, firm factors will provide greater explanation for their reasons to internationalize than will management, industry, regional environment, or host country factors.

Research Question #3. Do reasons for internationalization vary significantly by age of small business?

Young small businesses are characterized by a dominant role of the owner/founder in determining the direction of the business (Cooper, 1981; Churchill & Lewis, 1983). Research has shown that owner/founders are opportunity-driven and optimistic in the face of obstacles encountered in creation of their enterprises (Timmons, 1985). Managers in younger ventures will frequently be the founders, which in itself results in a different type of emotional investment (Bird, 1989). Strategies of young businesses are highly related to the background and experiences of the founder (Feeser & Willard, 1990), and particular product/market choices are often individualistic (Miller, 1983) and guided by the vision of the owner/founder (Cooper, 1981; Kao, 1989).

In established small businesses the role of the manager is less dominant and more detached (Churchill & Lewis, 1983). While the characteristics, values and skills of the manager of an established small business cannot be separated from the company's strategy (Hambrick & Mason, 1984), non-founders are better able to delegate responsibility and listen to subordinates than founders (Dean & Meyer, 1989). Hence strategies in an older small business are more likely to be the result of planning, market analysis, and outsider input (Robinson & Pearce, 1984; Eggers, Leahy & Churchill, 1994) than purely personal preference. Following this logic, the younger the business at internationalization, the more significant management factors will be as motivators for internationalization. It is therefore hypothesized that:

> *Hyp. 3#a*—Age when internationalized will be negatively associated with management factors.

Young small businesses are resource constrained and experienced employees, and capital (Churchill & Lewis, 1983; Cooper & Dunkelberg, 1986). As such, their goals will be to acquire resources rather than manage and control resources (Stevenson & Gumpert, 1985) and to establish market legitimacy rather than to expand and grow (Lippit & Schmidt, 1967). Similarly, younger small businesses lack a track record of experience and therefore will be less likely to have achieved a specific competitive advantage or clearly defined market position (Casson, 1983).

On the other hand, old small businesses will be more likely to have administrative procedures in place (Churchill & Lewis, 1983; Eggers, Leahy & Churchill, 1994), experienced employees, and resources (Cooper & Dunkelberg, 1986). These businesses will be more likely to have established some type of competitive advantage---brand name recognition, market position (niche), or proprietary technology.   As such, availability of resources or possession of competitive advantage would be logical reasons for internationalization of old small businesses (Dunning, 1980; Robock & Simmonds, 1983, Casson, 1986) and would be less likely for young small businesses. Given differences in the characteristics of these businesses based on age, it is expected that firm factors as reasons for internationalizing will be more prominent for old than young small businesses. In other words, the older the business at internationalization, the more significant firm factors will be as reasons for internationalizing. It is therefore hypothesized that:

> *Hyp. #3b*—Age when internationalized will be positively and associated with firm factors.

While young and old small businesses will be unlikely to have a dominant industry position due to their size disadvantage (Casson, 1983b) or to succeed internationally, performance aside, industry conditions such as intense competition, mature markets or slow growth may indeed motivate a small business to sell its products abroad. For young companies, owner/founders are less likely to be constrained by the perceived risks or barriers of an industry (Timmons, 1985). In fact, new firms are creating disequilibrium by their innovation and entry (Schumpeter, 1942). Nevertheless, no business has unlimited strategic flexibility in an industry environment (Harrigan, 1985). Still young firms are less constrained by these industry conditions and behave more aggressively than old firms that may be more set in their ways (Covin & Covin, 1990). Due to experience in the marketplace, old small businesses will be more likely to have established a niche or industry position. This experience will provide them with the benefit of information (organizational learning) and resources which will allow them to identify and respond to industry structure changes, competition, or growth. As reasons for internationalization, industry factors would therefore have a greater influence on old rather than young small businesses. In other words, the older the business, the more important industry factors will be as reasons for internationalization. It is therefore hypothesized that:

Hyp #3c—Age at internationalization will be positively associated with industry factors.

The characteristics of new small businesses, such as lack of formal systems, resources and structure (Churchill & Lewis, 1983; Kazanjian & Drazin, 1990), and less management time limits their ability to keep track of and analyze domestic conditions (Dollinger, 1985). Because of limitations, these businesses will have less capability to collect and evaluate information about foreign market opportunities and trade policies. On the other hand, old small businesses will have the advantage of operating experience, giving them first hand knowledge of the effects of domestic economic, demographic, and regulatory factors on their businesses. As such, favorable or unfavorable domestic conditions may be a likely reason for old small businesses to consider international expansion (Aharoni, 1966; Johanson & Vahlne, 1977). In addition, old small businesses will have the organizational structures and capabilities to collect information about international opportunities. Because of these differences, it would appear that perceptions of their immediate regional environmental conditions would be more likely to motivate old than new small businesses. In other words, the older the business at internationalization, the more significant regional environment conditions would be as a reason for internationalization. It is therefore hypothesized that:

> *Hyp. #3d*—Age at internationalization will be positively associated with regional environment factors.

Given that perceptions of international risk are related to experience in markets (Johanson & Vahlne, 1977), it is suggested that host country conditions affecting the decision to internationalize will be different for young and old small businesses. Young small businesses will lack information about market potential, size and distribution channels due to their lack of operating experience (Churchill & Lewis, 1983). As a result, their decision to sell products abroad will be more often based on the personal perceptions of opportunities or contacts of the owner/founder (Cooper, 1981) or unsolicited orders from abroad. Conversely, old small businesses will be more likely to cite reasons such as favorable market conditions, growth, or demand resulting from information obtained (Johanson & Vahlne, 1977; Thorelli, 1987). As theories suggest, the market experience of established small businesses will provide them with more information and knowledge of host country conditions (opportunities and barriers) (Johanson & Vahlne, 1977), and it is expected that older businesses will be more likely to cite host country conditions as reasons for internationalization than younger companies. It is therefore hypothesized that:

> *Hyp. #3e*—Age at internationalization will be positively associated with host country factors.

Research Question #4. What are the similarities and differences across new and established small businesses in their international strategies?

Both young and old businesses are constrained by their small size (employees) and lack of market power (Galbraith & Stiles, 1983; Casson, 1983b). As a result, horizontal integration or diversification will be difficult strategies for these businesses to implement. Even though there has been research that shows small businesses do invest directly in foreign countries, these small businesses are relatively few in number (Kohn, 1988; Oviatt, McDougall, & Dinterman, 1993). In other words, it is likely the most popular entry mode for these businesses will be exporting and that there will be no significant difference in foreign market entry mode based on age of internationalization of small business-es. It is therefore hypothesized that:

Hyp. #4a—Age will not be positively associated with any particular mode of entry.

Young small businesses are characterized by their lack of resources, both human and financial (Churchill & Lewis, 1983; Cooper & Dunkleberg, 1986), and a lack of market experience and product acceptance. As a result, it is less likely they will be able to make a significant commitment of resources or people in foreign markets. Furthermore, these same business characteristics suggest young small businesses will not have the capability to sell a wide variety of products in many countries or internationalize over a broad geographic area, focusing on a few countries with minimal commitment. On the other hand, the older a business is at internationalization, the more likely it will have higher degree of internationalization, wider geographic scope of operation, and greater commitment than younger small businesses. It is therefore hypothesized that:

Hyp. #4b—Age will be positively associated with degree of internationalization (commitment and geographic scope) in small busi-nesses.

A summary of all hypotheses are found in Exhibit #4.2. Expected outcomes of hypotheses testing are presented in Exhibit #4.3, 4.4 and 4.5. The next section discusses the research design that was employed in this investigation.

RESEARCH DESIGN

The goal of this research was to develop a descriptive scheme and explore possible relationships between variables (Denzin, 1978, pp. 58-63). The design selected was a non-experimental static group comparison survey, which is suitable for exploratory investigations where a phenome-non is to be described (Denzin, 1978). This design permitted a compari-son across two types of small businesses, young and old, at age of internationalization. A cross-sectional mail survey was the major source of data gathering.

This investigation was carried out in four phases: secondary research, pilot studies, and mail survey, and data analysis. Multiple methods of data gathering, or a hybrid methodology (Harrigan, 1983) utilizing some field interviewing, mail survey, and archival data collection was employed. A hybrid methodology allows for more generalizability, as well as for more detailed observations and interpretation of individual experiences (Harrigan, 1983).

Exhibit #4.2

RESEARCH QUESTIONS AND HYPOTHESES

Research Question #1. What factors motivate the decision of young small businesses to engage in international business activities?

> *Hyp. 1-* In young small businesses, management factors will provide greater explanation for their reasons to internationalize than will firm, industry, regional environment, or host country factors.

Research Question #2. What factors motivate the decision of old small businesses to engage in international business activities?

> *Hyp. 2-* In old small businesses, firm factors will provide greater explanation for their reasons to internationalize than will management, industry, regional environment, or host country factors.

Research Question #3. Do reasons for internationalization vary significantly by age of small business?

> *Hyp. 3a-* Age at internationalization will be negatively associated with management factors.

> *Hyp. #3b-* Age at internationalization will be positively associated with firm factors.

> *Hyp #3c-* Age at internationalization will be positively associated with industry factors.

> *Hyp. #3d-* Age at internationalization will be positively associated with regional environment factors.

> *Hyp. 3e-* Age at internationalization will be positively associated with host country factors.

Research Question #4. What are the similarities and differences across young and old small businesses in their international strategies?

> *Hyp. #4a-* Age at internationalization will not be positively associated with any particular mode of entry.

> *Hyp. #4b-* Age at internationalization will be positively associated with degree of internationalization (commitment and geographic scope) in small businesses.

Exhibit #4.3

EXPECTED IMPORTANCE OF FACTORS MOTIVATING THE DECISION TO INTERNATIONALIZE BASED ON COMPANY AGE

Factors	*Hypothesis #1* Young	*Hypothesis #2* Old
Management	+	
Firm		+
Industry		
Regional Environment		
Host Country		

****

Exhibit #4.4

EXPECTED RESULTS FROM HYPOTHESES TESTING FOR SIMILARITIES AND DIFFERENCES IN REASONS FOR INTERNATIONALIZATION BASED ON COMPANY AGE

Contextual Factors	*Business Age*
Hypothesis 3a- Management	negative
Hypotheses 3b- Firm	positive
Hypothesis 3c- Industry	positive
Hypothesis 3d- Regional Environment	positive
Hypothesis 3e- Host Country	positive

Exhibit #4.5

EXPECTED RESULTS FROM HYPOTHESES
TESTING FOR SIMILARITIES AND DIFFERENCES
IN INTERNATIONAL STRATEGIES BASED ON COMPANY AGE

International Strategy	*Business Age*
Hypothesis 4a- Entry Mode	not significant
Hypothesis 4b- Degree of Internationalization	
Scope	positive
Commitment	positive

SAMPLING PLAN

To allow for maximum generalization, a national stratified sample was taken from several listings of small businesses. A national sample avoids any bias due to economic variations in certain areas of the country. Given the descriptive nature of this study and need for wide geographic diversity, stratification was chosen as an efficient means to achieve proportional representation (Kidder & Judd, 1986) across the various geographic regions of the U.S. The sample was stratified based on the ten Small Business Association geographic regions.[1] This stratification was an acceptable means to achieve geographic representation and deemed to be a reasonable way to identify differences in the population before sampling (Fowler, 1988).

A second consideration taken into account for sampling was the present age of the businesses. Because the focus of this study was age at internationalization, and there was no way to determine this from any of the published lists, a higher proportion of young internationalized businesses were sampled. It was felt that this additional stratification would insure a high enough response by young internationalized businesses to allow for comparison to the old group.

The sample was composed of 1076 internationalized small manufacturing businesses which were identified from six different published lists (see Appendix B for a description of these publications). The reason for this diversity in lists was to avoid sample bias which could occur when relying on one list, and because there is no single comprehensive listing of internationalized small businesses. Moreover, there was no accurate count of the total number of small manufacturers that are internationalized. The SBA (1986) estimated approximately 90,000 to 100,000 small businesses were engaged in exporting (*Report to the President*, 1988), but these numbers do not distinguish between service and manufacturing firms. However, using the estimate of 100,000, this represents approximately two percent of the five million small business establishments[2] (*State of Small Business*, 1990). If we estimate that the proportion of the 485,274 small manufacturing establishments involved in international business are the same as above, we can estimate that approximately two percent of the these, or 9,705 small manufacturing establishments, are internationalized. Using these estimates, this study will survey about eleven percent of the total number of internationalized small business manufacturing establishments. (See Exhibit #4.6.)

Identification of small businesses by age has been done frequently in the field of entrepreneurship research (Sandberg, 1984; McDougall, 1987). However, there is wide variation as to what age constitutes new. The range is five years (Slevin & Covin, 1987; Goslin, 1987) to twelve years (Slevin & Covin, 1989), with the majority of studies using eight years or less (Sandberg, 1984; McDougall, 1989). Consistent with research using the SBA data base (Kirchoff & Phillips, 1988) and other studies (Fredriksen, et al, 1989; Brush & VanderWerf, 1992; Brush & Peters, 1992), it was decided to use six years as the cut-off between young and old.

The size criteria for the sample was consistent with the U.S. Office of Management and Budget classification, where small businesses are identified as those having less than 500 employees (see footnote number two, Introduction). The decision to limit this sample to non-diversified independently-owned small businesses is consistent with other research where the objective is to maintain some homogeneity in a sample (Sexton & VanAuken, 1984; Denzin, 1978). Other researchers in the field of Entrepreneurship have followed this practice (McDougall, 1987; Slevin & Covin, 1989; 1990; Feeser & Willard, 1988; Brush & Peters, 1992).

There are several precedents in entrepreneurship research for selecting samples using published directories such as *Dun and*

Exhibit #4.6

ESTIMATED POPULATION OF
INTERNATIONALIZED SMALL BUSINESSES

Estimated number of small
    businesses establishments in U.S.*   5,004,336

Estimated number of small
    manufacturing establishments**   385,247

Estimated number of internationalized small
    manufacturing establishments***   9,705

Number of internationalized small manufacturing
    establishments surveyed in this research   1,076

*-*State of Small Business*, 1990, p. 82, based on 1986 estimates

**-*State of Small Business*, 1990, p. 82

***- An estimate, based the number 100,000 internationalized small businesses, as a proportion of the number of small business establishments, which is two percent. It is estimated the proportion of internationalized small manufacturers would be the same.

Bradstreet's Directory (McDougall, 1987) or the *Corptech Directory* (Keeley & Roure, 1989; Tyebjee, 1990). Because there is no single published listing of internationalized small businesses, the decision was made to use multiple directories to identify a sample for this research.

In order to be sure the respondent group included small businesses that had internationalized at an early age, all new businesses that could be identified were surveyed. Old businesses were randomly chosen by selecting one business per every three pages of each directory used (Fowler, 1988).

This research is limited to manufacturing firms for three reasons. First, it is more difficult to measure exchanges, firm-specific advantages and other international activities of service businesses. Second, statistics and records maintained by the Small Business Administration are more readily available for products than for services (*The State of Small Business*, 1989) and this allows for background and secondary information to be compared to primary data. Finally, small manufacturing businesses produce more jobs and produce more output per hour than small service businesses (*The State of Small Business*, 1989, pp. 42, 67). The choice of an all-multiple rather than few-industry study was made because it was anticipated that there might be too few internationalized small businesses that internationalized at an early age in any single or limited set of industries.

This sample is also limited to independent small businesses that are not part of larger organizations. This excludes new businesses started by larger parents and divisions or branches of large companies. It is expected that branches or divisions of larger companies will have greater access to financial, human, and informational resources. Hence, this study is deliberately narrowed to small independent manufacturers to provide some homogeneity within the sample (Ireland & VanAuken, 1987), and prevent against confounding of results possibly due to sectoral differences (service versus manufacturing) or resource base (subsidiaries versus independent companies).

SECONDARY DATA COLLECTION

In order to understand the general economy of the different U.S. SBA regions, background information total exports and top country of export by region, number exports and free trade zones were collected from secondary sources. These sources included industry experts, government officials, and published materials. The purpose of this data was to put the survey into context and allow for comparisons of results. This information is summarized in Appendix C-1.

Government officials and trade representatives were telephoned to inquire about policies and assistance for small firms that wished to internationalize. Major sources were the SBA, the Department of Commerce, and State Offices of International Trade. (This information is summarized in Appendices C-1 to C-4.)

Recent statistics show that eighteen federal agencies are involved in export promotions while twenty-three state governments are spending $50 million a year supporting twenty-seven technology extension centers (Penner, 1992). Despite these extensive programs, only one half of the potential users are aware of the export promotion programs and only one in four actually use them (Seringhaus, 1991). Services most frequently offered include marketing, procedures and documentation, publicity, direct training, product adaptation and guidance for financing (Seringhaus, 1991).

State level initiatives generally are designed to create awareness of international opportunities. These programs focus on specific industries, such as computer or seafood, or particular countries. For example, the Bureau of Domestic and International Commerce (BDIC) in Pennsylvania, a state subsidized agency, has established offices in Japan and Europe to promote exports. These offices abroad seek to identify competition, evaluate market information, and establish contacts for small businesses. An official of BDIC notes;

> "Small businesses are sometimes reluctant to deal with government agencies because of the bureaucracy. Government agencies often lack visibility for their positive efforts, and could use a more effective marketing strategy."

Some states such as Illinois are cutting back on export promotion activities due to budget constraints. These cutbacks would appear to hurt U.S. small businesses abroad. The National Association of Manufacturers notes that the U.S. spends 50 cents per capita on export promotion compared with four dollars in France and five dollars in Japan (Penner, 1992, p. 70).

The Small Business Foundation of America is one of many new associations founded to assist small businesses. A representative of SBFA stated:

"Businesses do not perceive information about foreign markets accurately, but see risks and more management work when this is not necessarily the case. The visibility of resources and information provided by government agencies is poor---more marketing of programs is needed."

This official indicated that lack of financing and information were the two most common problems, while the development of a central government information system was the most frequent request by companies in the organization.

General information about host country conditions was also collected. Favorable and less favorable market and business opportunities for small businesses were reviewed by using expert sources and periodicals from both the Organization for Economic Cooperation and Development (OECD) and the World Bank. Both organizations frequently collect this type of data. The countries accounting for the most growth in foreign exports are noted in Appendix C-5).

PILOT INTERVIEWS

The purpose of the pilot interviews was to refine constructs and to examine their validity (Kidder & Judd, 1986). The intent was to assess how well the items (variables) measured the constructs (Zeller & Carmines, 1980, p. 78). Specifically, factors leading to international business activity and types of international business activity were explored. These interviews served to test questions for understandability and to narrow the scope of this investigation by eliminating variables of peripheral importance. Methodology employed followed field research techniques to the extent that the conceptual framework proposed was verified (Kidder & Judd, 1986, p. 180). Businesses selected for this phase were chosen for their representativeness in terms of age and geographic location. Five pilot interviews were conducted: three with businesses that internationalized within the first six years, and two with companies that had internationalized at a later age. These manufacturing companies were selected from different industries and ranged in size from 45 to 300 employees, and in gross revenues from $700,000 to $35 million. These interviews were conducted either in person or by telephone and lasted between ninety minutes and two hours. Questions were unstructured and non-disguised. (See Appendix D for brief description of each of the companies interviewed in these pilot interviews.) (Exhibit # 4.7 reflects a summary of the main findings of these studies.)

Pilot interviews were used to identify important factors motivating internationalization, and to eliminate variables. Variables were eliminated if they were not affirmed as important or did not appear to vary widely by age at time of internationalization. On the other hand, new variables were added. For example, two of the businesses noted relationships with customers and clients were quite important. The president of a microfiche products manufacturing company said: "Relationships are everything; reciprocity was a prime concern in our decision to internationalize". A similar comment was made by the president of an electronic dermatology products manufacturer who stated his personal experiences and contacts were factors in the decision to sell products abroad.

Exhibit #4.7

SUMMARY FINDINGS FROM PILOT INTERVIEWS
n=5

1. Main reasons for internationalization:

    . to create or maintain personal relationships
    . the opportunity offered itself
    . lack of competition in product/market abroad
    . always intended to sell products abroad

2. How implemented international strategy:

    . entered single market
    . direct or indirect export

Another variable added was the intention to internationalize. Three of the five presidents stated that they had always intended to internationalize. For instance, the president of a twelve-year old computer software company that first sold abroad at age five stated: "I always envisioned my business as international from the start. In fact, the first employee I hired was a British citizen. I just wish our business had sold products abroad sooner than five years into our operations." This view was supported by a new manufacturer of electronic dermatology products. He said: "I knew there was a market abroad, and I never considered anything but international sales".

In this limited pilot sample, those that internationalized at a young age were strong in their statements about "opportunities". The president of a four-year old golf club company, that internationalized at age one, indicated the company internationalized when the "opportunity presented itself". Japanese buyers had requested they sell their golf products abroad. Likewise, the dermatology products manufacturer felt there was a big "opportunity in Europe" because the competition there was weak.

As far as international strategies were concerned, all the businesses began selling their products in a single market, and entered these markets by exporting. Two businesses exported directly and three exported through agents.

CROSS SECTIONAL SURVEY

A cross-sectional survey was the major method of data gathering. The survey was developed inductively, including some previously used measures and questions. Pre-testing was carried out to check the questionnaire for understandability and content validity (see Summary of Validity and Reliability Issues at the end of this chapter for further discussion). The instrument was tested on a group of six academic experts and three practitioners who reviewed and commented on the clarity, order of questions, comprehensiveness, organization, and overall presentation of the questionnaire. Based on recommendations and comments from this expert panel, revisions were made. After the revised questionnaire was completed by two of the pilot interviewees, these individuals were asked to evaluate the clarity, comprehensiveness and ease of answering the questionnaire. Revisions were once again made in the process consistent with survey research methodology (Fowler, 1988). (A copy of the final questionnaire is included in Appendix E-1.)

The final version of the questionnaire included questions covering four general areas: firm demographics (location, size, products, performance), factors affecting decision to engage in international business activity, types of international business activities, and opinions about regional environment and host country conditions. Multiple measures were used for each of the constructs noted in the conceptual framework

(Denzin, 1978). (A description of measures and operationalizations follows in the next section.)

Efforts to increase the response rate were taken by including a polite cover letter, offering to send respondents a copy of the summary results, and mailing of reminder postcards (Hinrichs, 1975) (see Appendix E-2 for copy of cover letter). To encourage a higher response, the questionnaire was mailed during a non-holiday period and return postage was pre-paid. The questionnaire was six pages long consistent with findings showing no differences between response rates for questionnaires four-to six-pages in length (Sheth & Roscoe, 1975). The survey was addressed to the president of the company. Previous studies have found that top executives have relevant information about the strategy of a business (Hambrick & Mason, 1984), and new venture researchers have followed this practices (McDougall, 1987).

An important issue for cross-sectional research is reliability or accuracy of the measuring instrument (Kerlinger, 1973). This can be accomplished by using the same measure on the same population at more than one point in time (Zeller & Carmines, 1980). In order to check for stability of answers over time, six completed questionnaires were randomly selected. About four months after their response was received, each of these respondents was telephoned and asked about their answers to the questions specific to the interest of this project. (Questions re-checked were #2, #3, #4, #8, #10, #11.) (See Appendix E-1, copy of Questionnaire.) In each case respondents were read the question, their response, and asked if this was what they meant, and if they had anything further to add. In all cases, there was no discrepancy between the written answer and the follow-up responses given by telephone (Fowler, 1988).

Another component of reliability is to evaluate the internal consistency of the measuring instrument (Kerlinger, 1973; Zeller & Carmines, 1980, p. 54). This is to determine the consistency of results across populations. The most popular techniques are split-half equivalent and Chronbach's alpha, the latter being more widely used and producing better results (Churchill, 1979). To accomplish this test, respondents may be split into early and late, or odd and even groups (Churchill, 1979). A high coefficient alpha indicates that the samples perform well in capturing consistency. For this research, the respondent group was split on an odd/even numbered basis, and the reliability test was run. The reliability coefficients ranged from alpha of .6036 to .9418. An item-to-item correlation of .5 to .6 or better, for early stages of basic research are agreed to be adequate measures of reliability (Nunnally, 1970; Churchill, 1979). This instrument met the criteria.

OPERATIONALIZATIONS AND MEASURES

Constructs and variables were operationalized using a combination of scaled, open, closed, dichotomous, and multiple answer questions. Because the purpose of this research was to differentiate between businesses based on age of the company, five-point Likert Scales were chosen for operationalization of several of the constructs (See Appendix E-1 for copy of Questionnaire.) Likert scales have the advantage of allowing for either positive or negative assessment of each item; are appropriate for assessing multiple aspects of the constructs being measured; can be factor analyzed; and are fairly easy for respondents to complete (Kidder & Judd, 1986). Furthermore, these Likert scales can be divided into subscales, that include two or more content domains (Kidder & Judd, 1986). Likert scales also permit the use of statistical procedures that can be applied to interval data (Nunnally, 1978; Kerlinger, 1973). For each of the main constructs noted in the conceptual framework (see Exhibit #4.1), multiple items were used to measure each of the variables. Exhibit #4.8 indicates the constructs, variables, operationalizations and question number, and type of measure used in this research.

Management factors were operationalized using three main variables: background, contacts, and views toward internationalization. Background consisted of work and travel experience (Bilkey, 1978), education (Simpson & Kujawa, 1978; Cavusgil & Naor, 1987), and business skills (Cavusgil & Naor, 1987). Consistent with work by Johanson & Vahlne (1977) and Cavusgil & Naor (1987), pilot interviews in this project showed that personal contacts either in the form of friends, relatives, or customers were important motivators in internationalization. The view of the manager towards internationalization was also deemed important in both pilot research and in previous empirical investigations (Perlmutter, 1969; Reid, 1984; Kedia & Chokar, 1985; Cavusgil & Nevin, 1984; Ursic & Czinkota, 1984; Lindquist, 1990). All management variables were measured by at least one five point Likert scale allowing respondents to rate the importance of these items in their decision to internationalize as well as either a second scaled or open question. Exhibit #4.8 contains a complete listing of the variables measured, sources, and the question from the survey containing the measure.

Firm factors were operationalized by three variables: characteristics, resources, and specific advantages. Firm characteristics such as age (Ursic & Czinkota, 1984; Welch & Weidersheim-Paul, 1980) and experience in domestic markets (Johanson & Vahlne, 1977), have been found to be important in the decision to internationalize. Resources such as trained employees (Tesar, 1977; O'Rourke, 1982), employees with international experience (Cavusgil & Naor, 1987), capital resources (Bilkey, 1978; Tyebjee, 1990), and information (Johanson & Vahlne, 1977; Bilkey, 1978) also are important motives for selling products abroad. Specific advantages also motivate internationalization and these are composed of patented product technology (Reid, 1979; Robock & Simmonds, 1983; Cavusgil & Naor, 1987); innovative products (Cavusgil & Naor, 1987; Ursic & Czinkota, 1984), and low production costs and economies of scale (Caves, 1982; Buckley, 1983) are factors in the decision. Cooperative arrangements (Marchesnay & Julien, 1990) are other forms of firm specific advantages), and customer service capability found important in pilot interviews, and were included. All firm variables were measured using open or multiple answer questions and five point Likert scales which asked respondents to rate their importance in the decision to sell abroad.

The issue of firm size has yielded inconsistent results as a motive for internationalization (Horst, 1971; Cavusgil, 1984; Caves, 1982). Research on small businesses has found that size doesn't directly motivate a company's decision to internationalize, however, internationalization is usually correlated with availability of resources (Reid, 1980; Cavusgil, 1984). In this investigation, the sample was limited to small businesses with less than 500 employees; variations may be reasonably expected in resource availability between businesses of twenty versus 499 employees. Hence, size in terms of number of employees (Caves, 1982) and sales (Cavusgil, 1984) during year one of internationalization were measured in open questions and considered in data analysis.

Industry factors were operationalized by a variable composed of industry characteristics, which included growth (Caves, 1982; Cavusgil, 1984; Johnson & Czinkota, 1985), competition (Vernon, 1983; Welch & Wiedersheim-Paul, 1980; Kothari, 1978), and structure (Dunning, 1979). Again these variables were measured using open questions, and five point Likert scales where respondents were asked to rate the importance of these variables in the decision to sell products abroad.

Regional Environment factors were made up of three main variables found by previous researcher's to motivate sales abroad; environmental conditions, resources, and market conditions. Environmental conditions were composed of economic conditions (Simpson & Kujawa, 1974), tax laws (Cavusgil & Nevin, 1984); access to port of exit, and distribution network (Tesar, 1977; Cavusgil & Naor, 1987). Resources were operationalized by foreign market information (Johanson & Vahlne, 1977; Bilkey, 1978; Thorelli, 1987); availability of capital resources (Bilkey, 1978); availability of experienced employees (Buckley & Casson, 1983); and availability of raw materials and supplies (Christensen, 1991). Market conditions included customer demand (Miesenbock, 1988), market size and growth (Buckley & Casson, 1983; Thorelli, 1987), and competition in home markets (Kothari, 1978). These variables were measured using five point Likert scales and an open question asking respondents to list the most important of these Regional Environment factors in the decision to internationalize. (See Exhibit #4.8 and Appendix E-1.)

Host Country Factors were composed of environmental conditions, resources, and market conditions. Consistent with findings from other studies host country environmental conditions included economic conditions (Goodnow & Hansz, 1972; Kindleberger, 1969; Kohn, 1988); tariffs and trade policies (Galbraith, et al, 1990; Kindleberger, 1969), language similarity (Goodnow & Hansz, 1972; Thorelli, 1987; Kohn, 1988), transportation system and distribution network (Johanson & Vahlne, 1977; Ursic & Czinkota, 1984); and geographic distance from the U.S. (Goodnow & Hansz, 1972; Kohn, 1988). Resources were composed of capital resources (Rugman, 1979; Bilkey, 1978; Dunning, 1980), experienced employees (Thorelli, 1987); and raw materials and supplies (Buckley & Casson, 1979; Dunning, 1980). Market conditions included costs to enter market (Ursic & Czinkota, 1984), size of market (Thorelli, 1987), growth of market and customer demand (Cooper & Klienschmidt, 1980); and number of competitors (Dunning, 1979; Rabino, 1980). These variables were measured using five point Likert scales and an open question asking respondents to list the most important of these home country factors, in the decision to internationalize (See Exhibit #4.8 and Appendix E-1.)

There are two aspects of international strategy: entry mode and degree of internationalization. Entry modes most frequently measured are exporting, licensing and other contractual relationships, and foreign direct investment (Buckley, 1989; Akhter & Friedman, 1989). Degree of internationalization has typically been measured as percentage of foreign sales to domestic sales (Kirplani & McIntosh, 1980). However, because this is only a single dimension of international involvement, this variable was measured in two ways: scope and commitment (Welch & Lousitarinen, 1988). Scope of activities included number and diversity of countries, percentage of total manufactured products sold outside the U.S. (McDougall, 1989), and percentage of total sales from outside the U.S. (Cavusgil, 1984). The level of commitment (Cavusgil, 1984) included percent of foreign to domestic sales (Caves, 1982) as well as percentage of resources employed (people [employees] (Vernon, 1983), and goals (time horizon, short or long term) (Thorelli, 1987). These variables were measured using multiple choice and open questions.

Exhibit #4.8

CONSTRUCTS, VARIABLES, OPERATIONALIZATIONS AND QUESTIONNAIRE ITEMS

Construct/Variables	*Operationalization/ Citation*	*Questionnaire Item*
MANAGEMENT FACTORS		
Background	work & travel experience (Bilkey, 1978) education (Simpson & Kujawa, 1978; Cavusgil & Naor, 1987) business skills (Cavusgil & Naor, 1987)	q #2 open q #13 scaled
Contacts	friends, relatives, customers (Johanson & Vahlne, 1977; Cavusgil & Naor, 1987)	q #2 open q #13 scaled
Attitude	view of internationalization (Perlmutter, 1969; Bilkey, 1979; Reid, 1984; Cavusgil & Nevin, 1984; Kedia & Chokar, 1985; Lindquist, 1990	q #2 open q #14 scaled
FIRM FACTORS		
Characteristics	age (Ursic & Czinkota, 1984) experience (Johanson & Vahlne, 1977; Welch & Weidersheim-Paul, 1980)	q #2 open q #12 scaled
Resources	trained employees (Tesar, 1977; Caves, 1982) employees with international experience (Cavusgil & Naor, 1987) capital (Bilkey, 1978; Tyebjee, 1990) information (Bilkey, 1978; Johanson & Vahlne, 1977)	q #2 open q #12 scaled

FIRM FACTORS (continued)

Construct/Variables	Operationalization/ Citation	Questionnaire Item
Specific Advantages	patented product technology (Reid, 1979; Robock & Simmons, 1983; Cavusgil & Naor, 1987; Baird, Lyles, & Orris, 1994 innovative products (Cavusgil & Naor, 1987; Ursic & Czinkota, 1984) low production costs (Caves, 1982) economies of sale (Caves, 1982; Buckley, 1983)	q #2 open q #12 scaled
	cooperative arrangements (Marchesnay & Julien, 1990; pilots) customer service capability (pilots)	q #2 open q #12 scaled

INDUSTRY FACTORS:

Industry Characteristics	growth (Caves, 1982; Cavusgil, 1984) competition (Vernon, 1963; Welch & Wiedersheim-Paul, 1980; Kothari, 1978; Adams & Hall, 1993) structure (Dunning, 1979)	q #2 open q #12 scaled

REGIONAL ENVIRONMENT
FACTORS:

Environment Conditions	economic conditions (Simpson & Kujawa, 1974) tax laws (Cavusigil & Nevin, 1984) access to port (Cavusgil & Naor, 1987) distribution network (Cavusgil & Naor, 1987, Tesar, 1977)	q #2 open q #7 scaled q #8 ranking

REGIONAL ENVIRONMENT FACTORS: (continued)

Construct/Variables	Operationalization/ Citation	Questionnaire Item
Resources	foreign market information (Johanson & Vahlne, 1977; Bilkey, 978; Thorelli, 1987) capital (Bilkey, 1978) experienced employees (Buckley & Casson, 1983) raw materials & supplies (Christensen, 1991)	q #2 open q #7 scaled q #8 ranking
Market Conditions	customer demand (Miesenbock, 1987) size (Buckley & Casson, 1983; Thorelli, 1987) growth (Buckley & Casson, 1983; Thorelli, 1987) competition (Kothari, 1978; Cavusgil & Naor, 1987)	q #2 open q #7 scaled q #8 ranking

HOST COUNTRY FACTORS:

Construct/Variables	Operationalization/ Citation	Questionnaire Item
Environmental Conditions	economic conditions (Goodnow & Hansz, 1972; Kindleberger, 1969; Kohn, 1988; Galbraith, et al, 1990) tariffs & trade policies (Kindleberger, 1969; Galbraith, et al, 1990) language (Goodnow & Hansz, 1972) transportation systems (Ursic & Czinkota, 1984) distribution network (Johanson & Vahlne, 1977; Ursic & Czinkota, 1984) geographic distance (Goodnow & Hansz, 1972; Kohn, 1988)	q #2 open q #3 open q #9 scaled q #10 ranking
Resources	capital (Rugman, 1979; Bilkey, 1978; Dunning, 1980) experienced employees (Thorelli, 1987) raw materials & supplies (Buckley & Casson, 1979; 1983; Dunning, 1980)	q #2 open q #3 open q #9 scaled q #10 ranking

HOST COUNTRY FACTORS (continued):

Construct/Variables	*Operationalization/ Citation*	*Questionnaire Item*
Market Conditions	costs to enter (Ursic & Czinkota, 1984) size (Thorelli, 1987) growth (Cooper & Klienschmidt, 1991) customer demand (Cooper & Klienschmidt, 1981) number of competitors (Dunning 1979; Rabino, 1980)	q #2 open q #3 open q #9 scaled q #10 ranking

INTERNATIONAL STRATEGY
FACTORS:

Mode of Entry	export, license or contract, direct investment (Buckley, 1989; Akther & Friedman, 1989)	q #3b multiple choice
Scope	number of countries where product sold (Thorelli, 1987) percent total manufactured products sold abroad (McDougall, 1989)	q #4b open q #4c open q #20b open
Commitment	number of employees abroad (Vernon, 1983) goals (Thorelli, 1987) percent total sales from abroad (Cavusgil, 1984; Geringer, et al, 1989)	q #19c open q #15 open

VALIDITY AND RELIABILITY ISSUES

Reliability and validity issues were dealt with in various ways. While some of these issues have been mentioned earlier, this section will summarize reliability and validity concerns and indicate action this research has taken to deal with each of these issues. (Exhibit #4.10 reflects this summary.)

(1) External validity is an issue of concern when a researcher is unable to sample the entire population (Payne, 1973). In this investigation there was no single listing of internationalized small businesses. Therefore, six different listings were sampled in order to prevent list bias (Denzin, 1978). In order to insure the sample was representative geographically, it was stratified based on the ten SBA regions (Fowler, 1988).

To guard against sample bias, testing was done to insure that non-respondents were not significantly different from those businesses that did respond. First, a sample of thirty non-respondents and thirty businesses not surveyed were identified from the six listings. Archival data, including number of employees, age, sales, number of employees, percentage of international sales, product type, and scope of international sales, was obtained from the same directories as was identified in the mail sample. Thirty respondents were randomly identified, and the same data was extrapolated from list data. Chi-square tests were run to see if there were any significant differences among these groups across key dimensions (Fowler, 1988; Johnston & Czinkota, 1982; McDougall, 1989). (See Exhibit #4.9.) Results of these tests showed that there were no significant differences between these three groups on key dimensions. The p value for all tests was greater than .15, well above the .05 standard by which most results are regarded significant (Stevens, 1986).

Exhibit #4.9

RESULTS OF X^2 TESTS FOR NON-RESPONSE BIAS AMONG THOSE COMPANIES SURVEYED, NOT SURVEYED, AND NOT RESPONDING

Variable	X^2	Sig.	d.f.	n=
Date of establishment[1]	6.658	.1551	4	88
Port shipped from[2]	13.732	.1856	10	90
Number of countries[3]	2.822	.2439	2	41
Revenue category[4]	.045	.9770	2	34
International sales category[5]	1.621	.7432	2	39
Employee size category[6]	2.821	.2822	2	84

[1] The majority of all businesses were established post 1970 (49%).

[2] Ports of exit were grouped by region—West, Midwest, Northeast, Southeast, Gulf, and Great Lakes (Faucett, 1985).

[3] Forty-eight percent of the businesses in the combined groups sold products to five or less countries, while 25% sold to six to ten countries, and only 26% sold products to more than ten countries.

[4] Directory information on sales is generally given by category and as such tests were done for differences by category. The average revenues were less than $10,000,000, the highest company sales was in the less than $50,000,000 category.

[5] International revenues are generally categorical, and this data was less frequently available for all three groups.

[6] The average number of employees for all groups was 100. The range was 1 to 431.

Exhibit #4.10

SUMMARY OF VALIDITY AND
RELIABILITY ISSUES

ISSUE:

External Validity - when sampling an entire population is not possible, steps must be taken to ensure that the sample is representative of the population to which the researcher wishes to generalize (Denzin, 1978).

ACTION AND RESULTS:

> Randomly identified companies from 5 different lists; stratified sample based on 10 SBA geographic regions. Compared samples of non-respondents (n=30), businesses not surveyed (n=30), and respondents (n=30) across key characteristics such as sales, size, number of countries, and age. No significant differences were found in Chi-square tests.

ISSUE:

Convergent Validity - evidence from different sources gathered in different ways (Denzin, 1978).

ACTION AND RESULTS:

> a. Different Sources- Supplemented mail survey with expert opinions, archival data, and telephone follow-up to six respondents.

> b. Multiple Measures- Multiple measures of each construct included in questionnaire (Denzin, 1978). (See Appendix #E-1.)

> c. Multiple Methods- Research design included pilot interviewing (n=5), mail survey (n=134), and telephone interviews of respondents, experts and non-respondents. (Denzin, 1978; Harrigan, 1983).

Exhibit #4.10 (continued)

ISSUE:

Content Validity - Degree to which the item measures what it is supposed to; proportion of variance observed scores share with true score (Zeller & Carmines, 1980).

ACTION AND RESULTS:

> Pilot interviews (in-depth) with five companies; pre-tested survey instrument on six experts and three respondents. Many of measures previously used by other researchers.

ISSUE:

Construct Validity - Degree to which the theory behind the construct is explicated (Kerlinger, 1973).

ACTION AND RESULTS:

> Constructs accounting for business internationalization identified from theories; hypotheses developed and empirically tested (Zeller & Carmines, 1980, p. 81).

ISSUE:

Reliability - The degree to which independent researchers applying the same operational definition to the same sense data can concur in their determinations (Payne, 1973, p. 3).

> a. Stability Test- Retest of questions on six respondents at two different points in time (Nunnally, 1970; Kerlinger, 1973, p. 43).

> b. Equivalence- Chronbach's alpha testing -- separated sample based on odd/even number respondents (Nunnally, 1970; Kerlinger, 1973). Results of this testing showed satisfactory reliability with alpha levels of .6750 to .9489, satisfactory for early stages of research.

To further rule out any possible non-response bias, a random sampling of eight non-respondents not included in the archival data analysis were contacted by telephone. Of these eight: one was no longer in business, three didn't remember receiving any survey, two were no longer selling abroad, and two were too busy or out of town when the survey arrived and one "never got around to it". While in conversation with these business managers, inquiries were made about their total sales, number of employees, extent of international sales, industry type, and port of exit. These businesses (n=6) averaged less than 100 employees, their sales ranged from $100,000 to $10,000,000, and they exported to an average of five countries. These results are consistent with the archival data gathered for respondents, non-respondents, and those surveyed (Exhibit #4.9).

Other questions were asked regarding sales in international markets and reasons for internationalization. It might be assumed that non-respondents were less successful (profitable) than respondents. This did not appear to be the case; three indicated they were planning to expand international operations, and the other three were "doing fine". One non-respondent exporter of packaging materials to Europe stated; "American products have much credibility abroad. We are planning to establish direct manufacturing operations in the Philippines". As to reason for internationalization, this owner noted "An English company found us. Then after our initial success in Europe, we attended trade shows to establish distribution in the Pacific Rim Countries". A second company that manufactured aircraft propellers and parts indicated that more than forty percent of total company sales came from abroad. This company internationalized sixty years ago when foreign buyers approached them.

Seven companies that were not surveyed and not included in the archival data analysis were randomly identified from directories and telephoned: one was not presently internationalized; one received less than one percent of total sales from international markets; and the five remaining companies, the average number of employees was less than 100, sales ranged from $500,000 to $11,000,000, and they exported to an average of six countries. One president of man-hole drilling equipment began exporting to Israel in 1965, and then to Mexico, "because the markets had less competition". In all, this qualitative data supported the results of the secondary data analysis confirming no difference between respondents and non-respondents.

(2) Convergent Validity is the extent of agreement to evidence gathered in different ways from different sources. This is referred to as "multiple triangulation" (Denzin, 1978). In this research, the mail survey was supplemented with expert opinion from government and trade officials. The telephone survey to six respondents, eight non-respondents, and seven companies that were not surveyed. A second step taken to improve convergent validity was to include multiple methods of data gathering, in this case, the mail survey was supplemented by telephone pilot interviews and follow-up and archival data gathering. The data gathered from these various sources and methods was consistent.

(3) Content Validity is the degree to which a questionnaire measures what it is supposed to measure (Zeller & Carmines, 1980). Not only were previously used measures were employed and pilot interviews and testing of the survey instrument were accomplished on nine experts and respondents before the final survey was mailed.

(4) Construct Validity is an indicator of the degree to which the theory behind the construct is explicated (Kerlinger, 1973). To insure this constructs were identified from theories and operationalizations from previous research were utilized. Hypotheses were developed and empirically tested (Zeller & Carmines, 1980). (See Chapter V for results of hypotheses testing.)

(5) Reliability is the degree to which the construct is accurate. In other words, fellow researchers should be able to independently apply the same operational definition to another similar population and achieve similar results (Payne, 1973). There are two aspects: *(a) stability* and *(b) equivalence*. Stability measures is determined by testing and retesting of measures at two different points in time. This was done on a sample of six respondents and no variation in responses was noted. Equivalence refers to the internal consistency of measures and is tested using the Chronbach's alpha reliability statistic. The alpha levels were satisfactory.

SUMMARY

A conceptual framework derived from an integration of theoretical and empirical work in international business and entrepreneurship served as a basis for this research. Four sets of hypotheses were developed to test the effect of age in the small businesses internationalization decision. The research design included pilot studies and a cross sectional mail survey. The sample was composed of a nationally representative cross-section of internationalized small manufacturers. Sample stratification based on the ten SBA geographic regions was used. Secondary data was collected to provide context for this research. Constructs were operationalized using previously used measures. Finally, several steps were taken to insure reliability and validity in this research.

NOTES

1. Regarding sample stratification, the Small Business Administration has classified small business activity in the U.S. into ten regions (see for example, *The State of Small Business*, 1990, Appendix, A). To insure adequate geographic representation, questionnaires were mailed to each of the ten regions identified by the SBA.

2   The SBA defines establishments as those businesses with a single physical location (*State of Small Business*, 1990, p.82). Establishments differ from enterprises which may be an aggregation of many establishments. It is estimated that the majority of all establishments employ less than 500 employees

V

Data Analysis and Results

This chapter presents the data analysis and results of the mail survey to more than 1000 internationalized U.S. manufacturers. The response rate and descriptive statistics are followed by a discussion of hypotheses testing, and statistical analysis used to investigate relationships between internationalization and age at the time of the decision. This chapter does not present inferences or interpretation of results, rather it only describes results of statistical tests. Interpretation and discussion of the results, and relevance the literature is presented in Chapter VI.

RESPONSE RATE

Questionnaires were mailed in two waves: 1,064 in the first mailing and 216 in the second, for a total of 1,280. Of these, 204 were returned as bad addresses, bringing the total surveyed to 1,076 (See Exhibit #5.1). The number of usable responses was 134, a response rate of thirteen percent. While this rate is lower than planned, it is the modal response rate for mail surveys (Erdos, 1970). Also, as noted in Exhibit #4.6, this research surveyed approximately fifteen percent of the estimated total number of internationalized small manufacturing establishments (7,093). This group of 134 is approximately two percent of this population. Nevertheless, tests for non-response bias were taken to insure the respondent group was not different from non-respondents or those not surveyed across key dimensions. (See Chapter IV).

Exhibit #5.1

SUMMARY RESPONSE RATE

Summary	Mailing #1	Mailing #2	Total
Mailed	1064	216	1280
less bad addresses	176	28	204
Total	888	188	1076
Responses	112	22	134
Percentage response	12.6%	11.7%	12.5%

As noted in Chapter IV, this sample was stratified in order to achieve geographic representation. The response rates by SBA region are shown in Exhibit #5.2. This reflects the response rate by region as well as the share of U.S. enterprises by region.

This exhibit verifies the geographic representation of the research. The proportion of responses from most regions (i.e. Midwest, Northeast) is consistent with the breakdowns of enterprises by SBA region (*State of Small Business*, 1990, pp. 114-120). The higher proportion of responses from Region I is likely due the fact that the survey was mailed from a university in Massachusetts.

Besides being representative by region, responses were received from forty-eight states, the highest response rate being from California (n=23) and the second highest from Ohio (n=12). These states have a very high proportion of small businesses. According to SBA information, California has the highest number of small business establishments in the country (*Business America*, 1992).

As noted in Chapter IV, a higher proportion of new internationalized businesses (less than six years old today) were sampled to insure adequate representation of companies that had sold products abroad at a young age. Of the 1280 total surveyed, 269 (twenty percent) were less than six years old today. The second mailing was composed of a slightly higher proportion of new businesses than the first mailing. Of the entire respondent group, twenty-three businesses were less than six years old, and 111 businesses older than six years old in 1990. Although there is no government data on small businesses that categorizes internationalized businesses by age, it is presumed that this respondent group has a slightly higher proportion (seventeen percent) of new businesses than may exist nationwide.

Exhibit #5.2

RESPONSE RATE BY SBA GEOGRAPHIC REGION
COMPARED TO TOTAL SHARE OF U.S.
ENTERPRISES BY REGION

Region	Number/% Responses	No. U.S.*	Percent of U.S.*
I- CT,ME,MA, NH,VT,RI	22 /16%	213,124	5.5%
II- NY,NJ	11/ 8%	442,245	11.4%
III- DE,DC,MD, PA,WVA,VA	9/ 7%	356,733	9.2%
IV- ALA,FL,GA,SC KY,MISS,NC,TN	13/ 10%	601,569	15.7%
V- IL,IND,MI, OH,MN,WISC	27/ 20%	710,965	18.5%
VI- AR,LA,NM, OK,TX	9/ 7%	466,066	12.1%
VII- IA,KS,MO,NE	5/ 4%	207,317	5.4%
VIII-COL,MT,ND, SD,WY,UT	8/ 6%	150,120	3.8%
IX- AZ,CA,HA,NV	23/ 17%	543,361	14.2%
X- AK,ID,OR,WA	7/ 5%	161,752	4.2%
Total	134/100%	3,853,262	100.0%

SAMPLE CHARACTERISTICS

This section briefly describes the characteristics of the businesses at the time they internationalized and today. For all questions, frequencies, means, modes, and other statistics were evaluated.

The average current age of businesses responding to this survey was thirty years old. The year of establishment ranged from 1852 to 1989, the mode being 1985, median 1966 and mean 1960. Thirty percent of the companies had been started after 1980 and thirty percent between 1960-1979.

Since the goal of this research was to compare businesses by age at internationalization, it was important to be sure that the sample was representative depending on time of internationalization. In the sampling process it was not possible to identify the age at which businesses first sold products abroad. However, when surveys were returned, respondents were separated into groups of early (internationalized at 6 years or less of age) and late (internationalized at seven or more years of age). Surprisingly, the groups were nearly equal-sized--the early group totalled sixty-nine, and the late group totalled sixty-five.

Size of business was controlled for because only businesses of less than 500 employees were surveyed (see Chapter IV for discussion of research methodology). Small Business Association data indicates that the majority of small businesses have less than 100 employees (*Small Business in the American Economy*, 1990). The median number of employees in 1990 for the respondent group was thirty-five, the average being seventy, and the range was 1 to 450 employees. Eighty percent of the businesses had fewer than 100 employees. This is consistent with SBA statistics and does not differ significantly from the number of employees in those businesses not surveyed and not responding. (See Chapter VI, for a complete discussion.)

An examination of the size of the businesses based on number of employees at the time of internationalization showed companies were generally smaller at the time of internationalization. The average number of employees for this sample was forty, the median being fifteen, with the range being one to 400. Fifty percent of the respondents had fewer than fifteen employees, and ninety percent of the businesses employed fewer than 100 people at the time they first sold products abroad. Nevertheless, the majority of these businesses added employees after internationalization. In 1990 their average number of employees was seventy-eight, with fifty percent having less than forty.

Sales of these businesses in year one of internationalization ranged from $2,000 to $100,000,000, with the average being $4,607,089, the median $500,000 and the mode $5,000,000. Percentage of revenues from international sales ranged from one percent to ninety-nine percent. The mean was fifteen percent in year one, and in 1990 the mean was twenty-three percent. Gross sales in 1990 for the respondent group ranged from a low of $1,000 to a high of $210,000,000, the median being $2,250,000, and the average being 10 million. Eighty percent of the businesses had gross revenues of less than $10,000,000. This again is consistent with SBA statistics for small businesses (*The State of Small Business*, 1990, p. 157) which showed a high percentage of small businesses have revenues of less than $20,000,000.

Businesses in this research were also classified by a two digit SIC code consistent with other studies (Faucett, 1988). The results show a wide variety of industries were represented, with the highest responses in electrical and electronic equipment (17%), primary metals (13%), and miscellaneous manufacturing. (Exhibit #5.3 reflects the breakdown by industry.)

Exhibit #5.3

RESPONDENTS CLASSIFIED BY
TWO DIGIT SIC CODE

CATEGORY	SIC CODE	NUMBER	PERCENT
Food-kindred Products	20	10	7.5
Textile Mill Products	22	1	.7
Apparel-Fabric	23	3	2.2
Lumber-Wood	24	6	4.5
Furniture Fixtures	25	3	2.2
Paper and Allied Products	26	4	3.0
Chemicals-Allied Products	28	11	8.2
Petroleum Refin. Products	29	1	.7
Rubber-Plastic	30	4	3.0
Leather-Leather Products	31	4	3.0
Stone-Clay-Glass-Concrete	32	2	1.5
Primary Metal Industry	33	3	2.2
Fbrictd Metal Products	34	19	14.2
Machiny Except Electric	35	7	5.2
Electrical-Electronic	36	24	17.9
Transportation Equipment	37	4	3.0
Intrmnts, Photo, Medic	38	11	8.2
Misc. Manufacturing	39	17	12.7
TOTAL		134	100.0

Respondents were asked to describe their major industry of operations and a very wide range of industries were represented. Businesses
operated in industries ranging from biotechnology to dairy products to
sporting goods. The most frequently mentioned were the computer
industry (9%, n=12). Health care, including chemicals and phar-
maceuticals and telecommunications tied for second mention (7.5%,
n=10), with fashion and construction products being third most popular
(6.7%, n=9). (See Appendix C-2 for comparison to top five industries of
export for all businesses [large and small] in the U.S.)

Respondents were involved in manufacture of a wide variety of
products, ranging from equipment that drills the holes in bowling balls,
to de-hydrated spices, to medical testing equipment, and aircraft jet
engine parts. In accordance with work by other researchers, products also
were classified into two technology categories, high tech and low tech
(Stuart, 1992). High technology products included electronics (software
& computers), advanced materials, test measuring equipment, chemicals,
photonics and optics, telecommunications, and subassemblies and
components). Low technology products included any other products not
identified in the above categories. In this research, twenty-eight percent
were classified as high technology, and seventy-two percent were low
technology, which is not significantly different than small business
manufacturers nationwide.

In examining international business activities of the sample, the years
of internationalization ranged from 1920 to 1991. The form of internationalization was predominantly exporting---ninety-six percent. Of these,
sixty-eight percent (n=90) exported directly and twenty-eight percent
(n=36) exported indirectly through a broker or agent. The remaining four
percent were engaged in licensing or direct investment with only one
business noting it had invested directly abroad.

In the first year of internationalization, sixty-seven percent sold
products in one to two countries, twelve percent sold products in three to
ten countries, and four percent sold products in eleven to thirty countries.
The average of number of countries served in the entire sample was three
countries. The percentage of total manufactured products sold abroad
varied from less than one percent to ninety-nine percent, the average
being fifteen percent. More than seventy-five percent shipped less than
ten percent of their products abroad.

By way of comparison, the average number of countries where
products were sold in 1990 increased from three to fourteen. At this time,

only ten percent served two or less countries, with fifty three percent selling products in three to ten countries. Likewise the percentage of total manufactured products sold abroad increased to an average of twenty-three percent with only forty percent of the companies shipping less than ten percent of products, and seventy-five percent shipping one third of their products or more.

Most popular geographic regions countries for export were predominantly European,(42%), with Canada and Mexico a strong second (25%), and Asia third (10%). Canada was the country most often exported to in the first year of internationalization (21%, n=28), followed by England (16%, n=22), and Japan (12%, n=16). For eighty-one percent of the respondents, the first country of internationalization in year one was an industrialized nation with seventeen percent exporting to less developed, and two percent shipping to newly industrialized countries. (See Appendix C-5 for comparison to countries reflecting the most growth in U.S. exports.) Ports most often shipped from were on the East Coast (thirty-six percent): New York was most popular (thirteen percent), with Los Angeles and San Francisco being used by thirty-five percent of the companies. (See Appendix C-3 for comparison to for trade zones and ports by SBA region.)

The respondents were asked in an open question why they decided to internationalize. The most frequent response was to fill a customer request (24%). (Exhibit #5.4 lists the most frequently mentioned reasons for selling products abroad.) It should be noted that these answers are often difficult to interpret because of respondent phrasing. As a result, key words were identified such as market or customer when data was coded.

Exhibit #5.4

REASONS FOR INTERNATIONALIZATION

Reason	percent	number
Fill customer request	24%	32
Increase sales and profits	14%	19
Broaden markets	13%	18
Personally knew market existed	12%	17
Demand for product	6%	8
Followed customer	5%	6

For example, one manufacturer of golf clubs stated: "We were approached by a rep who assured us good volume and good margins." Similarly, a chemical manufacturer noted: "We were asked by an international customer to sell abroad."

When respondents were asked why they selected the particular country where they first sold their products, the answers were consistent with those in Exhibit #5.5. Thirty-three percent indicated that "the customer selected us." The results of the answers to this question are reflected below.

Exhibit #5.5

REASONS WHY SELECTED COUNTRY

Reason	percent	number
Customer selected company	33%	41
Demand for product	13%	16
Easiest	7%	9
Geographically close	6%	7
Similar language	5%	6
Trade regulations	5%	6
Personal contacts	5%	6

A typical response to the question of why the business selected a particular country, is reflected by this data product manufacturer: "We didn't pick them, they picked us."

Respondents also were asked to indicate the biggest obstacle encountered in the internationalization process. While there was a wide variety of obstacles noted, ranging from unreliable intermediaries,— customs, marketing requirements, and electronic conversion standards, the most frequently mentioned problems were financially related (12%, n=15). Exhibit #5.6 reflects the most often mentioned problems encountered in internationalization.

Exhibit #5.6

BIGGEST OBSTACLES ENCOUNTERED IN
INTERNATIONALIZATION PROCESS

Reason	*percent*	*number*
Costs/financing	12%	15
Marketing	7%	9
Government regulations/policies	7%	9
Lack of industry knowledge	7%	9
Developing contacts	6%	8
Foreign country trade policies	6%	8

Respondents were asked questions about their background, education and previous work experience. Nearly all of the respondents were involved in executive management, with ninety-eight respondents (73%) holding the title of president, owner, or CEO. Of this sample, sixty-two (48%) were involved in the founding of the company. For all but one of these individuals (n=61), it was their first entrepreneurial experience. All of the founders had previous experience in the field of their business, the average number of years being fifteen. Sixty-seven of the respondents had personally invested in the business, the average amount being $10,000 and the mode being $20,000. Similarly, fifty-four percent had controlling interest in their business, the average share held being sixty-two percent.

The age of individuals completing the survey ranged from twenty-five to eighty-eight, the average was forty-eight years. Eighty-seven percent were males (n=115) and thirteen percent (n=17) were female. The number of years education ranged from ten to twenty-three, the average being four years of college. Forty-four (34%) of the respondents had some education beyond college. The most popular fields of study varied from Liberal Arts, to Health Care to Physics. The most frequently mentioned area of study was business (33%, n=39), the second Engineering (27%, n=32), and third Liberal Arts (16%, n=19). Notably, only one respondent had a degree in International Relations.

Ninety-nine percent were U.S. citizens, although three were born abroad. The previous occupation of these respondents was varied from college professor, to military, to fashion coordinator. Most frequently mentioned were executive (17%, n=19), general management (15%, n=17), sales (11%, n=12), and engineer (10%, n=11).

HYPOTHESES TESTING

The hypotheses developed in Chapter IV examine differences between the small businesses in the sample based on age at the time of internationalization. To test these hypotheses, statistical tests including frequencies for the total sample, frequencies for each group (those that internationalized at six or less years of age and those that international- ized at seven or more years of age), Pearson's Correlation analysis, and Discriminant Function analysis were run. Following is a discussion of the statistical tests employed for each hypothesis.

Hyp. #1- In young small businesses, management factors will provide greater explanation for their reasons to internationalize than will firm, industry, regional environment, or host country factors.

As discussed earlier, it was expected that management factors would be most important to businesses that internationalized at an early age. To evaluate this, respondents were grouped into two categories: by age of internationalization six or less years and seven or more years[3]. Separate frequencies were run for each group to examine the importance of various factors in the decision to internationalize. Only the most important reason (factor) per respondent was noted. For the group aged six or less years at internationalization, the total number of cases for which there was complete data was sixty-nine. The answers to question #2a, inquiring why the company first decided to sell products abroad, are shown in Exhibit #5.7.

Exhibit #5.7

REASONS WHY SOLD ABROAD—Less Than
Six Years Old at Internationalization

Reason	number	percentage
To fill customer request	13	20%
Personally knew market existed	13	20%
To increase sales and profits	9	14%
To broaden markets	7	11%
Demand for product	6	8%
Opportunity	5	7%
Personal contacts	4	6%
Other*	9	14%
Total**	66	100%

* -Other-- n=2 or less per item, reasons included; previous experience, Why not?, followed customer, industry growth, defend competitive position, easier to sell products abroad

** -There were three cases missing answers to this question, n=66.

These results show that customer request (19%) and personal knowledge of market (19%) were the two most popular motives noted, while increasing sales and profits, and broadening markets were second and third most frequently noted. Comments that reflect the typical responses of young companies' reasons for selling abroad are:

"...[B]ecause I was familiar with the overseas market, and because I had an inquiry from overseas."—Manufacturer of saw chains

"...[W]e were approached by international customers. The domestic market was dominated by the 'Big Guys', and there was genuine managerial interest in the rest of the world."—Chemical manufacturer

To test the hypothesis, frequency distributions by factor category were examined and statistical tests were run. Responses categorized to represent management, firm, industry, regional environment or host country factors. Categorization was made by the primary researcher who evaluated responses to the open question. (See Exhibit #5.8.) The criteria for category assignment was based on whether explicit mention of management, company, industry, regional environment, or host country reasons. These category assignments were reviewed by a research assistant who independently grouped the same answers. The few disagreements were discussed and re-grouped.

Exhibit #5.8

REASONS WHY SOLD ABROAD BY CATEGORY—
Less Than Six Years Old at
Internationalization

Category	Number	Percent
Management	22	33%
Company	17	26%
Industry	2	3%
Regional Environment	3	5%
Host Country	22	33%
Total	66	100%

The frequency distribution indicates that management and host country factors contributed equally to motivating these young businesses to sell products abroad. Personal knowledge of the market and contacts were as important as host country factors. Statistical analysis using a X^2 test for uniform distribution, confirms this with a significance level of .000 and X^2 value 30.730 which indicates the reasons given are not likely to occur with equal frequency. Based on the frequency distribution, and the X^2 test, it is evident that management factors were not significantly more important that any of the other factors (regional environment, host country, industry, firm). Hence, hypothesis #1 can only be partially supported.

> *Hyp.# 2-* In old small businesses, firm factors will provide greater explanation for their reasons to internationalize than will management, industry, regional environment or host country factors.

This hypothesis addresses the major factors motivating old businesses greater than seven years of age to internationalize. To evaluate this, frequencies were run separately for this group. The total number of cases for which there was complete data was sixty-nine. As in the case with the early group, answers to question 2a, inquiring why the company first decided to sell products abroad, were evaluated (see Exhibit #5.9.)

The most frequently mentioned reasons in order of mention given by established businesses for internationalization were: to fill customer request, to broaden markets and to increase sales. Respondent answers representative of these reasons include:

> "We internationalized to increase our company's sales and meet demand for our product."—Manufacturer of western belts

> "The customer required the equipment unit and came to us by way of reputation."—Manufacturer of electron linear accelerators

Exhibit #5.9

REASONS WHY SOLD ABROAD—
More Than Seven Years Old at Internationalization

Reason	Number	Percentage
To fill customer request	16	30%
To broaden markets	10	19%
To increase sales and profits	8	15%
Followed customers	4	7%
Personally knew market existed	3	5%
To develop new market	3	5%
Demand for product	2	4%
Other*	8	15%
Total**	54	100%

*- Other—n=one per item, to develop greater market presence, why not?, industry need, opportunity, better prices.

**- There were fifteen cases missing answers to this question, n=54.

Exhibit #5.10

REASONS WHY SOLD ABROAD BY CATEGORY—
More Than Seven Years Old at Internationalization

Category	Number	Percent
Management	6	11%
Company	25	46%
Industry	3	6%
Regional Environment	0	0%
Host Country	20	37%
Total	54	100%

To test the hypothesis, frequency distributions by factor category were examined and statistical tests were run. Responses were categorized to represent management, firm, industry, regional environment or host country factors. Categorization was made by evaluating responses to the open question by the primary researcher. (See Exhibit #5.10.) The criteria for category assignment was based on whether the reasons explicitly mentioned management, company, industry, regional environment, or host country variables. These category assignments were reviewed by a research assistant who independently grouped the same answers. The few disagreements were discussed and re-grouped.

The most frequent responses by category were company related, with host country reasons being second. Statistical analysis using X^2 test for uniform distribution showed a significance level of .000 at X^2 28.709, indicating the reasons are probably not likely to occur with equal frequency. Given that the highest number of responses were company related, there is plausible support for this hypothesis. These data suggest firm factors provided more explanation for reasons to internationalize in the older group than management, industry, regional environment, or host company factors.

In order to examine hypotheses #3a to #3e, which compare small businesses by age of internationalization, Pearson's correlation tests were run. This test measures the strength of a linear relationship between two variables. A perfect positive linear relationship has a coefficient value of +1, and a perfect negative relationship has a value -1. Cause and effect relationships cannot be assumed from this test, only the strength and direction of a relationship. The significant results of these tests are presented in Exhibit #5.11.

Hyp. #3a- Age at internationalization will be negatively associated with management factors.

As discussed in Chapter IV, it was expected that management factors would be negatively and significantly associated with age at internationalization. Exhibit #5.11 shows seven management variables were negatively correlated with internationalization age, four of these significant at less than .05. These variables included customer contacts, friends, business associates, technical expertise, marketing expertise and experience in starting a new venture. While these correlations are significant, the strength of these associations is very weak suggesting a small but non-linear relationship between age and these variables.

Exhibit #5.11

RESULTS OF PEARSON'S CORRELATION ANALYSIS BETWEEN AGE AND MOTIVES FOR INTERNATIONALIZATION

Hypothesis	Variable	Sig.	Value
Hyp. #3a Management	q13a friends abroad	.024	-.2100
	q13b relatives abroad	.022	-.2179
	q13c business associate	.030	-.1975
	q13d customer contacts	.046	-.1734
	q13k technical expertise	.086	-.1438
	q13n experience starting new venture	.078	-.1522
	q13j marketing expertise	.083	-.1456
Hyp. #3b Firm	q11c long term relations	.068	.1435
	q11e overcome problems	.057	-.1552
	q12a trained employees	.069	.1405
	q12b emps. with int'l exp.	.056	-.1495
	q12d info. foreign market	.010	-.2542
	q12n high dom. profit & sales	.078	.1560
	q12o planning system	.076	.1448
	q12r flexible operations	.051	.1549
	q12s years exp. domestic	.031	.1761
	q12y innovative product	.059	-.1985
Hyp. #3c Industry	q12t in slow growing ind'y	.070	.1410
Hyp. #3d Regional Environment	q7c trade regulations	.034	-.1629
	q7f avail. exp'd emps.	.089	-.1389
	q7j home market growth	.069	-.1629
Hyp. #3e Host	q9e capital resources	.078	-.1932
	q9l transportation system	.013	.2826
	q9m distribution system	.007	.3192
Hyp. #4a Entry Mode	q3 entry mode	.311	.0513
Hyp. #4b Scope & Commitment	q4b1 number of countries	.107	-.1117
	q4c1 % total mfd. products	.060	-.1417
	q20b1 % total sales abroad	.010	-.2613
	q19c1 % total emps. abroad	.022	.3707

Given the presence of several significant and negative correlations, it is suggested that management factors are related to age as reasons for internationalization. As such, this hypothesis is supported.

Hyp. #3b- Age at internationalization will be positively associated with firm factors.

This hypothesis examines the relationship between age and firm factors. Results of the Pearson's correlation analysis show overall firm factors also are related to age. But once again even though the correlations are very close to .05 significance, the strength of the relationships is weak, with nothing stronger than .2542. (See Exhibit #5.11.) Six of the relationships are positive and four are negative with two significant at less than .05, and four at less than .059. These results show that age is positively and significantly associated with some firm factors, yet negatively and significantly related to others. While it was expected firm factors would be relatively more important in older businesses than younger, these results suggest different characteristics associated with age will motivate companies to internationalize. It was decided further statistical analysis was needed and this will be discussed in the next section.

As for support for hypothesis 3b, these mixed results do not allow for full support because some of the firm factors are positively associated with age and some are negatively associated. This hypothesis is partially supported.

Hyp #3c- Age at internationalization will be positively associated with industry factors.

This hypothesis suggests that business age will be positively related to industry factors as a reason for internationalization. Results of the Pearson's correlation are noted in Exhibit #5.11 and these indicate only one positive correlation of close significance (.07). While this is positive as expected, is a weak relationship (.1410) and the significance is not sufficient to support this hypothesis. This hypothesis is not supported.

Hyp. #3d- Age at internationalization will be positively associated with regional environment factors.

This hypothesis suggests that age will be positively and significantly associated with perceived favorability, or unfavorability, of regional environment factors (company's immediate environment) as a reason for internationalization. Results of the correlation analysis (shown in Exhibit #5.11), indicate there are three correlations, one of which was significant at the .05 level but all three of the relationships are negative. Contrary to expectations, regional environment conditions are more often associated with firm internationalization at an early age. These results do not support this hypothesis because all the relationships were negative.

Hyp. #3e- Age at internationalization will be positively associated with host country factors.

This hypothesis states that age will be positively associated with host country factors. Results of the Pearson's Correlation show three weak relationships, one of which is negative (capital resources) and not significant at less than .05. The positive associations are the two strongest correlations in the analysis with coefficients of .2826 for transportation system and .3192 for distribution system. In other words, businesses that internationalize late are more often concerned with host country conditions. As such, there is support for this hypothesis.

Hyp. #4a- Age at internationalization will not be positively associated with any particular mode of entry.

This hypothesis examines the relationship between entry mode and age. Results of the correlation analysis (shown in Exhibit #5.11) indicate there is not a significant relationship, the coefficient values being .0513 and significance level .3118. This result was as expected—mode of entry was associated with either a younger or older age. It is notable that since 126 of the 134 businesses exported, the only differentiation was between direct and indirect exporting. Again there were no differences between mode of entries by age and this hypothesis is supported.

Hyp. #4b- Age at internationalization will be positively associated with degree of internationalization (commitment and geographic scope) in small businesses.

This hypothesis refers to the degree of internationalization. As discussed in Chapter IV, it was expected that commitment and scope as measures of degree of internationalization would vary by age, with late internationalization being associated with greater commitment and scope.

(1) *Scope*—It was anticipated that geographic scope would be positively associated with age. Results of the correlation analysis show two correlations, neither of which are significant at less than .05. (See Exhibit #5.12.) Both associations were weak and negative. This infers that greater scope (number of countries) and percentage of manufactured products are associated with early internationalization rather than late. As such the hypothesis cannot be supported.

(2) *Commitment*—As in the case with scope, it was expected that greater commitment to foreign operations would be associated with businesses that internationalized later rather than early. Results of the correlation analysis show mixed results. While both correlations for percentage of total sales abroad in year one, and percentage of total employees abroad in year one are highly significant (.010 and .022 respectively) the strength of these relationships is greater than in other correlations. The former is negative and the later is positive. This suggests that later internationalization is associated with a lower commitment as represented by percent of international sales. On the other hand, percentage employees abroad is positively associated with older age as expected. As far as the hypothesis test, these conflicting results for commitment and geographic scope as measures of degree of internationalization do not allow support for the expected relationships.

In order to summarize the results of these hypothesis testing, Exhibit #5.12 indicates the degree to which the expected relationships were supported or not supported. To further analyze relationships between age and motives for internationalization, additional statistical tests were performed. These are described in the next section.

Exhibit #5.12

SUMMARY RESULTS OF HYPOTHESES TESTING

Hypothesis	Expected Relationship	Findings
Hyp.#1 Management factors will be most important for early internationalization	+	partial support
Hyp.#2 Firm factors will be most important for late internationalization	+	supported
Hyp.#3a Management factors will be negatively associated with age	-	supported
Hyp.#3b Firm factors will be positively associated with age	+	partial support
Hyp.#3c Industry factors will be positively associated with age	+	not supported
Hyp.#3d Regional environment factors will be positively associated with age	+	not supported
Hyp.#3e Host country factors will be positively associated with age	+	supported
Hyp.#4a Entry mode will not differ by age	+	supported
Hyp.#4b Degree of internationalization will be positively associated with age (scope & commitment)	+	not supported

RESULTS OF DISCRIMINANT FUNCTION
ANALYSIS

Given that there were several significant correlations, between age at internationalization and motives, it was decided that a Discriminant Function Analysis might offer greater explanation for any differences in reasons depending on age. A Discriminant Analysis is suitable for distinguishing between key factors that differentiate between two groups where a priori different groups are classified based on a set of independent variables (Morrison, 1969).

It is recommended that a hold-out sample of observation be withheld from the initial analysis to allow for subsequent tests of validity of the function. This allows for adjustment to upward bias that can occur if the cases used to compute the discriminant function are also used for the classification matrix (Klecka, 1980). However, given the relatively small size of the two groups and preliminary nature of this research, and being consistent with other researchers (McDougall, 1989), it was decided to use the entire sample in the analysis to be sure the coefficients were stable (Stevens, 1986). This suggests generalizability may be weakened, especially if the group classification is low. The method of extraction used was Wilks, a stepwise method that tests each variable by entering and removing them one at a time, minimizing the overall Wilks value of the function. This stepwise method tests each variable by entering and removing them one at a time. Selection and removal were based on tolerance (F-value) which is set a 1.0.

Keeping in mind the purpose of this study which was to determine which motives distinguish between those businesses internationalizing early and late, several steps were taken. First, the analysis was run with all variables that might potentially discriminate between the two groups. Given that there were eighty-eight variables, it was important to reduce the set to a smaller group of significant variables. To do this, the univariate F test of significance was run. F scores of all variables were examined. Only those variables that were significant at >1.0 were used in the analysis (Hair, et al, 1987), allowing only variables that would contribute to discriminating between the two groups to be in the analysis. There were 19 variables meeting this F-test. In addition, a correlation matrix was examined to be sure there was no multi-collinearity between variables. No variables had multicollinearity significant at less than p.10.

The results of the analysis will be discussed in three parts: overall function significance, the classification rate of the function, and the contribution of individual variables to the function.

Exhibit #5.13

RESULTS OF DISCRIMINANT ANALYSIS

Eigenvalue:	.3724
Canonical Correlation:	.5209
Wilks:	.7286
X^2:	39.4200
d.f.:	9.
sig.:	.0000

1. The function was highly significant. It would have been preferable to have a slightly higher eigenvalue, which is a measure of total association, however, the significance level and the high canonical correlation indicated there was a high degree of relatedness between the function and the two groups (Klecka, 1980; Stevens, 1986).

2. Given that the function was significant, the next step in interpretation was to determine how well the function classifies the cases. It is generally suggested that the classification rate should be at least twenty-five percent greater than would occur by chance alone (Klecka, 1980). For instance, considering a fifty percent classification by chance, the function should have a classification rate of at least 62.5%. There are two methods of determining the classification percent: the maximum chance criterion and proportional chance criterion. When group sizes are not equal, as in this study, the proportional chance is the suggested method to use (Klecka, 1980; Stevens, 1986; Hair, et al, 1987). For the proportional chance method the criterion value was computed by the following:

$$c \text{ proportional} = p^2 + (1 - p)^2,$$

where: p = proportion of total sample of individuals in group one

   $1-p$ = proportion of total sample of individuals in group two

In this case, group one was composed of sixty-nine cases, and group two was composed of sixty-two cases. The c proportional value was 50.49 percent, which means that the classification accuracy of the discriminant function must be greater than 50.49 percent to be higher than chance might allow. The classification process develops a matrix which indicated the prediction ability of the function. It is shown in Exhibit #5.14.

Exhibit #5.14

CLASSIFICATION MATRIX FOR DISCRIMINANT FUNCTION ANALYSIS

Actual	Predicted Group 1	Predicted Group 2
Group 1 = 69	47	22
Group 2 = 62	15	47
Ungrouped = 3		

Percentage of Cases Correctly Classified (hit rate) 71.76%

As noted above, the c proportional value used to evaluate the hit rate was 50.49 percent, and the hit rate well exceeded this criterion. As such, the predictive ability of the function in classifying the cases is very good.

3. Given that the classification rate met the test of prediction accuracy, it was meaningful to examine the individual standardized coefficient values of the nine variables that entered the function. (See Exhibit #5.15.)

The variables contributing the most to differentiating between the two groups (i.e. those with highest absolute value of the coefficient) were planning system, having friends abroad and years of experience abroad. Other important motives distinguishing between the young and old groups were employees with international experience, and ability to adapt to market changes.

Exhibit #5.15

STANDARDIZED COEFFICIENT VALUES FOR VARIABLES ENTERING THE DISCRIMINANT FUNCTION

Variable		*Coefficient*
q12o	planning system	-.6831
q12s	years experience in domestic markets	-.5434
q13a	friends abroad	.5483
q12b	employees with international experience	.4911
q12p	can adapt to market changes	.4836
q 7j	home market growth	.4276
q13c	business associates abroad	-.4223
q20b1	year 1 % international sales	.3723
q 4b1	total number of countries year 1 of sales	.2532

+ = group 1 (less than six years of age at internationalization)

- = group 2 (more than seven years of age at internationalization)

ANALYSIS OF PERFORMANCE

As noted in the methodology section discussed in Chapter IV, correlations were run to see if there were any associations between motives for internationalization and performance. Performance was operationalized using computed variables, growth in sales and growth in employees. These operationalizations are consistent with the most frequently used measures in the entrepreneurship field (Brush & VanderWerf, 1992). The results of this analysis are reflected in Exhibit #5.16.

Exhibit #5.16

CORRELATIONS BETWEEN MOTIVES FOR
INTERNATIONALIZATION AND PERFORMANCE

Growth in Sales

Variable	Value	Sig.
q7a Regional market econ. conditions	.2595	.018
q7k Regional market competition	.2044	.047
q12b Economies of scale	.2010	.051
q13c Business associates	.2188	.044
q13g Studied abroad	.2466	.030
q13h Lived abroad	.2185	.047

Growth in Employees

Variable	Value	Sig.
q7a Regional market econ. conditions	-.2613	.005
q7e Regional capital resources	-.1957	.026
q7f Regional experienced employees	-.1803	.040
q7g Regional raw mat'ls & supplies	-.1853	.035
q9l Host transportation system	-.1955	.028
q12d Foreign market information	.1974	.028
q12k Economies of scale	.2377	.011
q13e Foreign government contacts	.2495	.010
q13i Travelled abroad	.2422	.010

These tests show that growth in sales is significantly and positively related to three management factors; business associates, studied abroad and lived abroad. Economies of scale was the only company factor to reflect a relationship. Regional market competition was positively related while favorable economic conditions were negatively related to growth in sales.

Relationships between motives and growth in employees were different from growth in sales results, in that five of the nine significant correlations were negative. Four of the negative correlations were regional environment conditions—favorability of economic conditions, capital resources, experienced employees, and raw materials. Furthermore, host country transportation system also was negatively related. Two company factors reflecting a positive relationship were economies of scale and foreign market information. Similarly, two management factors were positively related; foreign government contacts and travel abroad. It is notable that the negative relationship between regional market economic conditions and growth in employees is highly significant, p. .005.

In addition to correlations between motives and performance, an analysis was run between age at internationalization and performance. The results of this test are noted in Exhibit #5.17.

Exhibit #5.17

CORRELATIONS BETWEEN AGE AT INTERNATIONALIZATION AND PERFORMANCE

Variable

Year 1	*Value*	*Sig.*
q19a1 year 1 total employees	.2227	.011
q19c1 year 1 total employees abroad	.3707	.022
q20a1 year 1 total sales	.0276	.406
q20b1 year 1 % sales international	-.2613	.010

1990	*Value*	*Sig.*
q19a3 1990 total employees	.1490	.099
q20a3 1990 total sales	.0112	.459
q20b3 1990 % sales international	-.3072	.004
q4c2 % product sold abroad today	-.2847	.001
Growth in sales (1990 sales - year 1 sales)	-.0106	.464
Growth in employees (1990 employees - year 1 employees)	-.0799	.207

In examining these correlations between performance and age at internationalization, it that businesses selling abroad are larger in number of employees. As for sales, total sales year one do not differ significantly depending on age at internationalization. Early internationalization is associated with a higher percentage of international sales. In 1990, there is no significant difference in relationships between performance and age at internationalization in total employees or total sales, except that younger age associated with a higher percentage of products and sales from abroad.

The correlations growth for in sales and growth in employees by age at internationalization were not significant. In other words, there is no apparent relationship between growth in sales or employees depending on age. This suggests that age at internationalization is not a factor in determining the overall performance of these small businesses.

ANALYSIS OF SIZE EFFECTS

It is important to determine that the effect of firm size does not confound the interpretation of results. Other researchers have indicated that size and age are related (Reid, 1980). Because older businesses that grow frequently have more resources and employees (Churchill & Lewis, 1983), it is possible that the reasons for internationalization may be explained by size and rather than age, if there are significant differences. To guard against mis-interpretation of results due to any significant size differences between the two groups, t-tests were run. The null hypothesis was that the means were likely to be equal—there is no significant difference between group one (early) and group two (late) based on employees and sales in year one of internationalization. If the observed significance value is .05 or less, one cannot confidently assume the means are not the same. The results of these tests are shown below in Exhibit #5.18.

This exhibit shows, the significance values for both sales and employees were not less than .05, suggesting that we cannot assume the means are not the same. However, we cannot assume the mean values are equal. The mean number of employees for young businesses was thirty, and for old it was fifty.In fact the businesses older at internationalization appear to be larger, but the difference according to the statistics is not significant. The same was true for sales in that the mean value for young firm sales was $3,890,948 and for old businesses was $5,540,242. Furthermore, correlations betweenage at internationalization size in year

Exhibit #5.18

RESULTS OF T-TESTS FOR DIFFERENCES IN COMPANY SIZE

	t-value	d.f.	2 tail prob.
Year 1 total employees	-1.50	105	.137
Year 1 total sales	-0.52	74	.604

Group means - Employees		*Group means - Sales in Year #1*	
Young =	30 employees	Young =	$3,890,948
Old =	50 employees	Old =	$5,540,242

one of sales abroad revealed a positive and significant relationship between employees and age (.2227, sig. .011) but no statistically significant relationship was apparent between sales year one and age (.0276, sig. 406). It should be noted that the SBA considers all businesses of less than 100 employees to be very small, and those of less than 500 employees to be small (see Endnotes, Introduction). This may imply that size differences among companies of less than 100 employees are less pronounced than differences between companies between less than 100 and more than 100 employees.

Even though the t-tests were not statistically significant, suggesting these two groups are not widely different, in order to be most confident that the relationships between age and motives were not being confounded by size effects, three additional steps were taken. First, correlation analyses were run using all the same motives used in the analysis of age at internationalization. These tests yielded only five motives that significantly (less than .05) correlated with the number of employees in year one of internationalization. (See Exhibit #5.19.)

Exhibit #5.19

CORRELATIONS BETWEEN MOTIVES FOR INTERNATIONALIZATION AND SIZE

Motive	*Sig.*	*Value*
q12a trained employees	.006	.2690
q12k economies of scale	.006	.2856
q12t in slow growing domestic industry	.010	.2520
q13b relatives abroad	.049	-.1925
q13k technical expertise	.010	-.2570

Of these correlations, only three showed up in the age analysis, relatives abroad, trained employees, and technical expertise. (See Exhibit #5.11.) Both of the latter two motives were more significantly related to age than size. These results show that between age and motives there are only three variables from the entire univariate analysis where size and age both matter. Furthermore, it also should be noted by the reader that the correlation between age and size was weak.

Second, to examine further the role of size as a possible confounding variable, both sales and number of employees in year number one of internationalization were included in the initial F-test for the discriminant function analysis. Sales year one had a very insignificant univariate F-value (sig. .7786), while employees was significant only at .2095. Because the criteria for inclusion in the final discriminant analysis was a significant F value of .05 or less (Hair, et al, 1987) these variables were not included in the final discriminant analysis.

Third, to take the analysis one step further, the best discriminant function was re-executed and size/employees year #1 of internationalization was added even though the variable technically did not meet the F-test criteria, (F value 1.591, p.2095). Size/employees year #1 did enter the equation, along with all nine of the same variables in the previous discriminant analysis. However, the addition of size (employees) did not improve the hit rate at all, and the canonical correlation improved only by .01. Hence the confounding effect of size in this analysis of age and motives is quite minimal. For only three variables is size a possible alternative explanation.

These tests suggest that, as expected, there are slight size effects; but age is more frequently and significantly related to motives for internationalization than size.

SUMMARY

This chapter presented the results of the mail survey of 134 internationalized small businesses. The response rate from the initial survey of 1,076 companies was thirteen percent. The survey was representative both geographically and by business sector. Data analysis included descriptive statistics, X^2 tests correlation analysis, and discriminant analysis. These statistical tests were used to evaluate hypotheses proposed in Chapter IV and assessed the relationship between age of internationalization and motives for selling products abroad. Overall, the results of the hypotheses were mixed: four were supported, two were partially supported, and three were not supported. Findings of the discriminant analysis indicated there were nine variables that contributed to a significant function which classified seventy-one percent of the cases accurately. Discussion and interpretation of these finding follows in Chapter VI.

NOTES

1. Age at internationalization was computed by subtracting the year of establishment from the year the company first sold its products abroad, q1c - q1a on questionnaire shown in Appendix E-2.

VI

Discussion of Research Findings

This chapter discusses the reserach results and offers interpretation of the findings noted in Chapter V relative to theories of entrepreneurship and international business, empirical studies, and secondary data. First, general results about reasons small businesses internationalize are presented; and second, similarities and differences by age are discussed. This chapter concludes with the limitations of this research with which any interpretation of findings must be considered.

GENERAL FINDINGS—COMPARED TO THEORIES

This book has argued that there are many possible motives may encourage small businesses to sell products abroad. The findings in Chapter V support this in that a wide range of motives were statistically significant. Elements from both international business and entrepreneurship theories were associated with internationalization in this study.

Behavioral Theories

These theories posit that internationalization will be motivated by the response to an opportunity, problem resolution, internal impetus or external threat. As noted in Chapter V, the most popular reason for selling products abroad was to "fill customer request". Similarly, the choice of a particular country of export was often determined because "the customer selected us". These responses appeared to be consistent with behavioral stream which suggests businesses will be motivated by the strength of an internal or external stimulus (Aharoni, 1966). This is similar to Reid (1980) and Suzman and Wortzel (1984) who argues that perceived "opportunity" is key to the decision to internationalize.

The importance of the executive and his/her leadership role in the decision process (Aharoni, 1966; Johanson & Vahlne, 1977) also is noted

115

in behavioral theories. This study found several businesses sold abroad due to "personal knowledge of markets" supporting the idea of managerial impetus. Relatedly results showed that the experience of the owner/-manager (travel and business skills) motivated internationalization, suggesting experiential learning is related to the internationalization decision (Johanson & Vahlne, 1977). However, given that some of these businesses were very young, it is likely the skills and knowledge obtained by the owner/manager did not result from experience with the present venture. This supports entrepreneurial theory which notes that the strategy of a new venture will be closely tied to the background and experiences of the owner/manager (Cooper, 1981; Vesper, 1990).

Consistent with behavioral theories, the first country where most these small businesses sold abroad was close, both geographically and culturally, to the U.S. (Johanson & Vahlne, 1977). Several respondents noted they selected the first country of export because it was "close" or had "similar language". This implies a more conservative strategy for these companies as opposed to a riskier approach of selling to distant and diverse markets.

In contrast to these supportive findings, the premise from behavioral theory that businesses must have operating experience and be established before exporting products abroad was not in evidence. Not only were several businesses currently less than six years old identified as internationalized, but also many respondents that were currently seven or more years of age had sold products abroad at an early age. There were twenty-one businesses, or sixteen percent of the entire sample, that were internationalized at start-up, and seventeen (thirteen percent) that internationalized within year one. Of the thirty-eight that sold abroad in year one or before, fourteen were identified in the original sampling procedures, but twenty-four of the companies sold abroad at an early age and were founded more than six years ago. This indicates that nearly twenty percent of businesses in this study that are "old" today (and thirty percent of the sample overall) internationalized very young in organizational life. This supports the proposition offered by McDougall (1989), McDougall, Oviatt & Brush (1991) and Oviatt & McDougall, (1994), that companies can be "global" from start-up. Furthermore, there were no significant differences in 1990 company sales or 1990 number of employees based on age at internationalization. This implies that success internationally can occur at any age, contradicting the assumption that due to a lack of experience, young firms will face greater risks and challenges and be unable to succeed.

Another contradiction to the stage model is the fact that thirty percent of this sample internationalized as a response to unsolicited orders. For these companies, this implies a more opportunistic, flexible strategic approach rather than rational, intentional and planned. These findings suggest that the stepwise process of internationalization (stage model) can be either speeded-up over a shorter period of time, or that businesses can leap-frog over different steps. Relatedly planning and experience were not rated as highly in the decision to sell abroad. Planning systems and years experience in the market (question #12, Appendix F-4)[1] had mean importance ratings of 2.8 (on a five point scale) or lower in terms of importance in the decision to sell products abroad. Instead of a planned, incremental stepwise process, this study reflects behavior reminiscent of Bygrave's (1989) chaotic theory of entrepreneurship where steps are skipped and the process is disjointed. In addition, this offers support for recent speculation that the stage model is too deterministic (Melin, 1992) and that companies do not always internationalize sequentially (Welch & Loustarinen, 1988).

Behavioral theories also assume that a companies are motivated to internationalize due to a desire to overcome or resolve organizational problems (Johanson & Vahlne, 1977). Respondents from this sample rated this reason fairly low (mean value 2.4 on the five point scale), compared to others, which indicates it was not a major motivation. As noted earlier, it was customer request (unsolicited orders) that caused the majority of these businesses to seek international sales, rather than the existence of a problem, lending support for Aharoni's (1966) premise that internationalization is not only problem driven, but may result from a positive stimulus.

Classical Theories

This stream from international business proposes that firms will search for new exchange opportunities while seeking profit maximization. Motives for internationalization (foreign direct investment) include limited exchange opportunities, structural conditions and industry factors. Even though these theories of the MNE were intended to apply to large established businesses, and this sample was composed of small manufacturers that exported, some of these classical motives were tested and found to be reasons for selling abroad. For instance, one of the responses to the open question asking why companies decided to sell products abroad was: "to increase sales and profits". Likewise, in question #11 (See Appendix F-3) which included reasons for internationalization, "to increase sales and profits" was very highly rated relative to other responses, the mean value being 4.41 on a five point scale. Other reasons noted in this question,—"to develop a new market" and "to seek large market share"—also are consistent with classical theory and had overall high ratings mean values of 4.24 and 3.4 respectively. Contrary to the intended application of classical theories, motives for increasing sales and profits, seeking exchange opportunities, expanding market share, and entering new markets were given as reasons for selling abroad.

Domestic "high growth in sales", domestic "high product acceptance", domestic "high profits" (from question #12, Appendix F-4) were not highly rated and did not appear to be important motives for internationalization in this group of small businesses. Similarly, industry factors such as "in slow growing industry", "large number of domestic competitors", and "intense domestic competition" were rated quite low overall by this sample (mean value of two or less). In other words, industry factors were relatively less important motives compared to the importance of management, regional environment, host and company factors. However, this generalized interpretation must be treated cautiously. This was a cross industry study and certain industry factors may be more or less important depending on the type, growth stage, and size of the industry.

Overall, some of the motives from classical theories do seem to apply in the context of small businesses. Perceived exchange opportunities, and goals for high profits and sales were reasons for selling products abroad. As noted above, the assumptions about market position and experience did not apply to the ability of these companies to succeed internationally. While this study did not include businesses that might have failed in internationalization, the fact that thirty percent of this sample sold abroad at less than six years of age, and had equal performance to those companies that sold abroad later implies that structural conditions (industry factors) may motivate companies to internationalize whether or not they are big or small, old or young.

Neoclassical Theories
These theories of foreign direct investment argue that a desire to seek cost efficiency and decrease risk will motivate internalization of specific assets. In this study, cost efficiency, or a goal of economizing on costs, was not noted in the open question as a motive for internationalization by any respondent. Reasons such as "low production costs" (2.7 mean value) and "economies of scale" (2.3 mean value) were comparatively low relative to others in question #12. (See Appendix F-4.) Given the small

size of companies in this sample (most had 100 employees or less), these results seem logical because they do not produce products on a grand scale. On the other hand, aspects of competitive advantage noted in question #12 (see Appendix F-4), such as "quality product", had a mean value of 4.0 (on five point scale) making it an important reason for selling abroad. Similarly, "to capitalize on domestic competitive advantage" was rated moderately important. These results imply that possession of a unique competence, or firm specific advantage (Hymer, 1960), will motivate small businesses to seek sales from abroad. While these companies were not internationalized by direct investment (horizontal or vertical integration), the possession of unique or specific advantages were important reasons for internationalizing. Hence proprietary asset advantages as motives for selling abroad are not necessarily contingent on size or age of company. Instead, young small companies with unique advantages may be motivated by these considerations as well.

Entrepreneurial Theory

Factors important in new venture creation include innovation, creation, risk-taking, and general management activities. Start-up strategy is a argued to be a function of identification and pursuit of an opportunity (Timmons, 1985). While responses to open questions were not intended to address motives for venture creation, many of the reasons for internationalization were quite similar to those important in venture creation. For example, nearly one third of the respondents indicated that the international "customer came to them". This suggests that these businesses took advantage of an opportunity when it was presented, then acted to fill the "gap" in the market (Liebenstein, 1968). This is consistent with Timmons (1985) and Stevenson and Gumpert (1985) who propose entrepreneurs recognize, seize and implement opportunities.

Several respondents noted that they sold abroad "to develop new markets", and that possession of "innovative products" were important to the decision. These reasons follow ideas about entrepreneurs creating and exploiting new markets, and innovating, all of which are essential to entrepreneurship. This finding suggests that entrepreneurial motives normally associated with the domestic context can apply in the international context as well.

Contacts and relationships were also very important reasons for the decision to internationalize, emphasizing the importance of the "general management" role of the owner/manager in the internationalization decision. In question #13 (see Appendix F-5), contacts with customers, business associates, were rated relatively high (mean values 3.5 or 3.75). Mitton, (1989); Aldrich, Woodward & Rosen, (1987); and Christensen, (1991) noted that it was "know who" that leads to "know how". In this case, contacts and relationships internationally were instrumental to the decision of many companies to sell products abroad, following entrepreneurship theories.

In general, these findings suggested that various aspects from all of the theories discussed in Chapter II help to explain the motives for small business internationalization. Consistent with previous research on exporting in small businesses, the behavioral theories seemed to offer greater explanation of the motives for internationalization than classical and neoclassical streams. Furthermore, this research shows that aspects of entrepreneurial theory apply in the context of the international expansion decision. Exhibit #6.1 reflects the motives noted from theories in Chapter II and includes a new column noting the motives for which evidence was found in this research.

GENERAL FINDINGS—COMPARED TO EMPIRICAL STUDIES

While this research differed from earlier studies in that it did not examine differences between exporters and non-exporters, several of the motives for small business internationalization were similar to those found in these studies. No previous study has examined age as a determinant in motives or strategies for internationalization. Age has been included as a descriptive variable. For instance, Christensen (1991) noted that fifty percent of the Danish firms in his sample exported within the first three years of operations. Similarly, work by Kirplani & McIntosh (1980) found no evidence that businesses internationalizing early were less successful than those that sold products abroad later, or visa versa. Oviatt, McDougall & Dinterman (1993) found that young companies selling in multiple countries were able to succeed with a "global" approach. This research supports the findings of these studies.

In support of Bilkey's (1978) early research, and other studies (D'Souza & Eramilli, 1990; Kaynak, 1990), this study also found unsolicited orders to be an important reason for deciding to sell abroad. Similar to Cavusgil & Naor (1987), this study also indicated that having personal contacts abroad was an important for selling abroad.

However, contrary to previous studies, there were other factors that did not appear to be as important in the decision. For example, capital resources (Tyebjee, 1990), trained and skilled personnel (O'Rourke, 1985), industry competition (Kothari, 1978) and experience internation-

Exhibit #6.1

SUMMARY OF FINDINGS OF MOTIVES TO
INTERNATIONALIZE FROM THEORIES

	Behavioral		*Classical*	*Neoclassical*	*Entrepr-eneurship*	*This Study*
	Export;FDI		*FDI;Divers-ification*	*Horiz./Vert. Integration*	*New Venture Creation*	
Motives						
Resolve problem, avoid risk	+	+		+	*	
Pursue oppty		+			*	F
Executive push		+			*	F
Profit		+	+		*	F
Political imperative			+		*	
Industry structure			+		*	
Economize on costs			+	+	*	
Competitive advantage			+	+	+	*
Spread risk			+	+		*
Innovation					#	F
Creation					#	F
Risk-bearing					#	
General management					#	F

+ - Motives for direct investment or exporting from theories of international business.
* - Motives from international business associated with small companies.
# - Factors in the decision to create new ventures.
F - General findings from this research.

ally (Telesio, 1979) were rated relatively lower than other motives (questions #11, #12). (See Appendix F-3, F-4.) These differential results may be a function of the disparate samples across studies. Studies operationalize size differently, a variety of country contexts were the source of data, and some studies focus on service companies rather than manufacturers.

GENERAL FINDINGS—COMPARED TO SECONDARY DATA

As noted in Chapter I, the government does not collect detailed information on the exporting activities of small businesses making it difficult to compare the results of this study to other statistics. However, a survey by the National Association of Manufacturers (NAM) (company sizes not distinguished) indicated that sixty-six percent of their respondents (1390 of 2105) sold products abroad. Of those that were internationalized, fifty-eight percent (n=880) derived less than five percent of their revenues from exporting, and only ten percent derived more than twenty-five percent of their sales from abroad. While percentage of international sales from this research was higher than the NAM Study, it might be explained by higher proportion of very small businesses (less than 100 employees) in this sample. Problems indicated in the NAM study were similar to those noted in this research: financing and costs, distribution and representation were common obstacles to selling abroad.

Studies by Cognetics, a small business research firm located in Massachusetts, indicated that the majority of small business exporters were very small (less than 100 employees), employed niche strategies, and used FAX machines for international business (reported in *Business Week*, April 13, 1992, p. 70). Furthermore, the most popular countries shipped to were Canada, Japan, Mexico, Germany, Great Britain and Korea, with the range in international sales being four to sixty percent, the average being twenty-six percent, which is closer to the results of this study. These are the same countries accounting for the highest growth in U.S. exports overall. (See Appendix C-5). The majority of the businesses in this sample employed fewer than 100 people, exported few products to a few countries, and selected countries that were culturally and geographically close.

SIMILARITIES AND DIFFERENCES BASED ON AGE
AT INTERNATIONALIZATION

In comparing the differences between old and young businesses at the time they sold products abroad, their characteristics tended to fit the profiles discussed in Chapter I. The young businesses were different from old in terms of reasons for internationalization, and management factors (personal experiences of the owner/manager) were relatively more important (see Exhibit #5.11 correlations) than other motives. This is similar to work by Feeser and Willard (1990), and Cooper (1981), which noted that start-up strategy of a new venture, in this case, international strategy, is largely influenced by the background of the owner/manager. Contacts, business associates, relatives, and friends were more often important to young businesses rather than old in the decision to internationalize, which supports work by Aldrich, Woodward & Rosen; (1987) in the entrepreneurial area.

On the other hand, as business age at internationalization increased, management factors, contacts, and skills assumed lesser importance as reasons for selling abroad. The results of Hypotheses #1, #2, #3a, and #3b bore this out in that reasons for internationalization in young businesses were predominantly based on the personal knowledge of the owner/-manager whereas for older businesses, company factors were more important. The correlation analyses showed that contacts and friends were associated with younger age at internationalization significantly, but not strongly. Hence friends and contacts are more often generally important to young businesses than old, but as a motive for internationalization are of only mild importance.

Differences in importance of company factors between young and old age at internationalization also existed. Aspects of competitive advantage,—such as innovative products (Namiki, 1988; McDougall, 1989; Robock & Simmonds, 1983)—were more often associated with younger than older businesses. This supports empirical work from international business which emphasizes the importance of proprietary assets (Buckley, 1983) in motivating internationalization (Bijmolt & Zwart, 1994; Aaby & Slater, 1989). Conversely, the importance of foreign market information also was associated with younger firms, supporting other studies (Cavusgil & Naor, 1987). It is interesting that competitive advantage (Hymer, 1960) and possession of foreign market information (Johanson & Valhne, 1977) were not associated with older businesses in this study, and theories proposing these motives were intended to apply to established firms.

Established planning systems, resources (trained employees, profits), and years experience in the market were associated with businesses that internationalized later in their operations (see Exhibit #5.11 correlations). This was expected because the life cycle literature indicates these will be characteristics of established businesses (Churchill & Lewis, 1983; see Chapter I). Similarly, findings for old companies support the contention of the stage model (Johanson & Vahlne, 1977), whereby firms will endeavor to gain experience, develop systems and acquire resources before considering internationalization. Businesses selling products abroad at an old age likely had a comparatively stable administrative structure and additional resources that facilitated internationalization. However, businesses young at the age of entry into foreign markets did not meet the conditions set by the stage model because they were inexperienced, instead having market knowledge about foreign markets that arose not from organizational experience, but from the experience of the owner/manager.

Ironically, existence of a written plan for international expansion did not differ by age at internationalization. Only 16 of the 134 respondents indicated that they had a written plan for selling products abroad. Once again, the serendipitous nature of the decision,—responding to customer orders—was characteristic of the a good percentage of the sample. Taking this one step further, this implies that strategy is emergent (Mintzberg, 1978), which is consistent with research on planning in small businesses (Sexton & VanAuken, 1984).

Regional environment conditions motivating internationalization seemed to support international business theory in that conditions, such as perceived favorable local market growth and trade regulations played an important role in the decision for both young an old businesses. Because old businesses had more experience and were better established in domestic markets, they would appear to be more capable than young firms in evaluating potential regional environment threats or opportunities. Therefore it was expected regional environment conditions would be more important to old companies. In contrast, it was the younger businesses for which perceived favorable or unfavorable regional environment factors were somewhat important. (See Exhibit #5.12 correlations.) The perceived favorability ratings varied by industry or region, but overall the sample perceived regional environment conditions were of lesser importance to younger firms.

Relative to the importance of perceived host country conditions, only the availability of capital resources was important to younger businesses. This follows entrepreneurial literature that posits new ventures will seek to acquire resources (Stevenson & Gumpert, 1985). However, the existence of transportation and distribution systems was highly significantly related to established businesses,consistent with previous empirical studies in international marketing (Tesar, 1977; Cavusgil & Naor, 1987). This suggests older businesses consider implementation of an international strategy as important to the decision. These results on importance of motives arising from regional environment and host country conditions, imply that overall, small companies internationalize generally as a result of internal factors. This supports work by Bijmolt & Zwart, (1994).

As expected, entry mode into foreign markets did not differ by age at internationalization, except that younger businesses more frequently exported directly and older companies more often exported indirectly, using a broker or agent. Young businesses adopted a "riskier" international strategy than older businesses, because they entered a larger number of countries and sold a greater percentage of their entire products abroad in year one—a broader and more committed international strategy. (See Exhibit #5.11 correlation analyses and Exhibit #5.15 discriminant analysis.) Furthermore, younger businesses had an average of twenty-three percent of total sales from abroad, while for older the average was only six percent. On the other hand, average gross sales for businesses selling abroad young was lower than for older companies. (See Exhibit #5.18.) This supports entrepreneurial theory in that entrepreneurial businesses are often characterized as being "risk-takers" that pursue opportunities compared to more established businesses that exemplify a conservative approach. Similarly, the international diversification literature would say spreading the risk, by serving more than one country, is an advisable strategy (LeCraw 1984). Old businesses were more often associated with a strategy that employed a greater percentage of employees abroad, consistent with the increasing commitment expected with more established businesses (Cavusgil, 1984).

Based on the analysis in Chapter V, Exhibit #6.2 summarizes the approaches to internationalization based on timing (early or late). This illustrates that early internationalization is more often associated with a

Exhibit # 6.2

SUMMARY OF APPROACHES TO INTERNATIONALIZATION
EARLY VERSUS LATE ENTRY

	Early	*Late*
Scope:	many countries distance from U.S.	few countries closer to U.S.
Commitment:	high percent of products sold abroad	low percent of products sold abroad
	sales abroad high percentage of sales	sales abroad low percentage of sales

deep/broad strategy where the companies sold to a large percentage of products to a large number of countries that were often a greater distance away. Later internationalization was more often associated with a shallow/narrow strategy where companies sold fewer products to fewer countries that were typically closer to the U.S.

Considering the discriminant function analysis and the correlations together, it is apparent that established systems, years of experience, and a conservative entry strategy were more often associated with businesses that internationalize at a later age which supports the stage model (Johanson & Vahlne, 1977). In contrast, businesses that sold abroad early in life were more often encouraged by friends, employees with international experience, an ability to adapt to market changes and adopted a more risky entry strategy, which supports the entrepreneurship literature (Cooper, 1981; Feeser & Willard, 1990). In spite of these differences in motives, the results of the performance analysis show that there was no significant relationship between 1990 sales and age at internationalization. (See Exhibit #5.17.) Similarly, age at internationalization was not significantly related to either growth in sales or growth in employees (Exhibit #5.17). These results imply that age is not related to success. In other words, performance is not negatively affected by the time in life that a business internationalizes. In sum, motives for internationalization

varied by age, but there was no relationship between age of internationalization and performance.

LIMITATIONS

As with any research, there were limitations to this study. Throughout this project efforts were made to minimize these limitations, but there
remain some issues that must be stated and kept in mind for any
interpretation of these findings.

This research had the advantage of allowing for objective responses
and generalizability due to the cross-sectional survey design. Convergent
validity was a threat (Denzin, 1978) because of the static nature of the
responses (measures at a single point in time) and reliance on a single
self-reporting source for each measure. However, to overcome this
limitation, it would have been necessary to have at least three sources for
each company. This was prohibitive and of questionable feasibility. Many
small firms typically have only one or two senior managers. Steps were
taken to overcome this limitation in that several businesses were
interviewed either in person (pilots) or by telephone. In addition, others
were contacted both by mail and phone to verify the responses and insure
temporal stability of response (Huber, 1985). (See Chapter IV, for a
complete discussion.) Based on these efforts, and considering the
exploratory nature of this study there was reason to be confident of the
validity of these results. Moreover plans for a future phase of this
research program will involve a field study of a limited number of
businesses randomly selected from this respondent group which will
allow for a second measure and second source of information.

Another limitation was the effect of business size in this analysis.
While every effort was made to ensure that explanations of motive for
internationalization were not being affected by size, the fact remains there
were very slight but not statistically significant differences in size
(employees and sales) simply because older firms tend to have grown
bigger. The t-tests, correlations and discriminant analysis all took into
account the effect of size, and it was found there was some very minimal
effect, although it could not be controlled for completely.

Perhaps the most serious limitation to this study was the response
rate, which was 13 percent. Although this matches the modal response
rate for mail surveys (Erdos, 1970), researchers typically like to receive
at least a thirty to forty percent response rate (Fowler, 1988). Several
steps were taken to promote a higher response rate including a polite

cover letter, follow-up postcards, pre-paid postage, and offer of results. Unfortunately, budget constraints did not allow for telephone calls before and after the mailing, which would certainly have improved the response rate (Fowler, 1988).

Another effect of the lower than planned response rate was inability to compare responses by the ten geographic regions. This also resulted in some generalization across perceived favorability and unfavorability of regional environment conditions. Moreover, perceptual rather than objective measures of industry factors also were used. An extension of this research will endeavor to survey more businesses by region to allow greater regional comparisons and to compare to objective industry data.

Precautions were taken to guard against response bias. First, a three group statistical comparison of companies surveyed, companies not surveyed, and companies surveyed but not responding (n= 30 in each group) was made across six key dimensions using secondary data. The results of this testing reflected no significant differences. (See Chapter IV.) Second, telephone follow-ups were made to non-respondents to insure they did not differ in terms of success (sales and profits) or motives for internationalization. This phone survey indicated respondents and non-respondents were indeed quite similar. Hence, in spite of the low response rate, there is reason to be confident that these results reflected the characteristics of the population of internationalized small businesses.

Other limitations included the retrospective recall nature of this study. Executives were asked to report on factors leading to a decision that they may not remember very well (selective recall) depending on the time that the decision was made. To help in overcoming this limitation, multiple measures were included in the survey instrument. Furthermore, this was an exploratory study designed to describe major factors of importance in internationalize and not intended to investigate the decision process. Therefore this limitation was not a major shortcoming. In addition, future research will include investigation of the antecedents to the decision to internationalize using field research methods.

It should be recalled that this study focused on businesses from a large industrialized country and generalization of findings to companies in small less developed or newly industrialized countries must be made with caution. Replication of this research in other settings is important for future investigation.

Finally, the respondent group was composed only of surviving businesses from a wide variety of industries. Although the decision to sample across industries was deliberate, the broad representation combined with the small sample size suggested that specific motives may vary by type of business. Once again, this will be investigated in future phases of this research.

In all, every effort was made to insure external and internal validity and prevent sample bias given the resources available for this study. However, given the limitations as noted above, the reader must keep in mind the above qualifications when interpreting these results.

SUMMARY

General findings about reasons that small businesses decided to sell products abroad relative to theories of entrepreneurship and international business, empirical studies, and secondary data were presented in this chapter. Similarities and differences by age at internationalization were discussed and limitations to this project were noted. These results imply that a broad variety of motives from various theories will help to explain why small business in general will sell products abroad. Young businesses had different motives from old businesses in that the experience and contacts of the owner/manager, competitive advantage, and foreign market information were more important. Businesses that sold abroad at an old age were more frequently motivated by established planning systems and profits from domestic sales. While the entry mode for nearly all of the businesses in the sample was exporting, younger businesses tended to export directly and shipped a higher percentage of their products to more countries: older companies more frequently exported indirectly and had more employees abroad. Hence approach to internationalization varied implying young companies adopted a riskier international strategy, and with old companies being more conservative. These differences in motives and international strategies were not associated with significant differences in performance.

NOTES

1. It should be noted that by design, there may be a higher proportion of young internationalized businesses in the sample than may exist in the population overall. This discussion and that hereafter concerning mean values should take this into account. However, as shown in Appendices F14,–F5, the ranking of variables by importance in the decision to internationalize are similar.

VII

Conclusions and Implications

This final chapter briefly reviews the purpose and description of this research. Following this summary, the major conclusions of this study and implications to researchers, practitioners and public policy-makers are noted. Finally, ideas for future directions in international entrepreneurship are offered.

SUMMARY OF RESEARCH

This study was inspired by the increasing number of new small businesses that are internationalizing from start-up. New businesses are increasingly important to the U.S. economy because of the jobs and innovations they produce. The SBA estimates that nearly 100,000 small firms are exporting their products abroad. However, data is not collected by age, and there continues to be limited information available regarding the motives or international strategies of internationalized small businesses. Moreover, the U.S. Government encourages small businesses to sell products abroad as a means of improving the balance of trade. As noted in the Introduction to this book, this research sought to provide information about internationalized companies that were young (arguably entrepreneurial) compared to internationalized companies that were old. Because old and young small businesses differ across four main dimensions—focus, organizational structure and systems, role of the manager, and resources—it was expected that these distinctions would make a difference in their motives and strategies for internationalization.

A survey of literature indicated that most theories from international business were intended to explain foreign direct investment behavior of large established firms and had not been tested in the context of small businesses. Many of these theories presumed that the business was established and experienced prior to internationalization, therefore not applying to young small companies. Theories from entrepreneurship explain factors contributing to new venture creation or the entrepreneurial behavior of small companies, but do not explicitly address international activities or contexts. Hence, an integration of theoretical factors from international business and entrepreneurship was used to explore the motives and international business activities of small businesses.

The literature review found extensive research about small businesses in the international marketing area, but this work focused predominantly on differences between exporters and non-exporters, and implications for export performance. Although age has been included as a descriptive variable, no empirical work considers its effect as an explanatory variable in distinguishing among motives or strategies for internationalization.

A conceptual framework integrating theories and empirical work from international business was developed. This framework included four major factors: management, company, industry, regional environment, and host country. Hypotheses relating to the age of the business at internationalization were developed consistent with previously described differences between young and old firms.

The sample chosen for this investigation was small manufacturers located across the U.S. The major method of data collection was a cross-sectional mail survey, and 134 companies responded. The purpose was to identify the factors that caused these small companies to seek revenues abroad, to consider the effect of firm age in this decision, and to test the applicability of theories of international business and entrepreneurship in this context. Several tests of reliability and validity were met including telephone follow-ups and a survey of non-respondents. Because the intent of this study was to answer questions, the next section restates the initial research and provides brief answers based on the findings.

Research Question #1. What factors motivate the decision of young small businesses to engage in international business activities?

Consistent with entrepreneurship theories, it was expected that the dominant role of the owner/manager would lead to higher importance of management factors rather than company, industry, regional environment, or host country factors. This expectation was confirmed in that the manager's personal knowledge of markets, personal contacts, and expertise were all rated highly by young firms as reasons for selling products abroad. However, the importance of management factors   was tied to aspects of the market in the host country—such as market demand and the unsolicited order by customers abroad. In other words, for young firms, perceived market opportunity and management factors operated together to motivate internationalization. These findings parallel early descriptive differences between new and established small companies as noted in Chapter I.

Research Question #2. What factors motivate the decision of old small businesses to engage in international business activities?

It was anticipated that company factors would be most important in motivating older businesses to sell abroad, given they had a track record of operations. This was the case in that company factors such as a desire to for expansion and growth dominated as motives for established companies. However, there were some established companies that similar to young companies, noted that "response to unsolicited order" was a major reason for internationalizing. This supports earlier empirical findings from international marketing.

Research Question #3. Do reasons for internationalization vary significantly by age of small business?

The findings of this research showed that indeed reasons for internationalization do vary by age of small business. Age distinguished between administrative and entrepreneurial behavior of internationalized companies. Early internationalization was characterized by predominance of management motives, supporting entrepreneurial theory which is characterized by innovative, opportunity-seeking behavior that manifested in the dominant role of the owner/manager. Young internationalized businesses were motivated by personal contacts, the expertise of the owner/manager, product innovation, and information about foreign markets. In addition perceptions of favorable regional environment conditions, such as availability of trained employees, regulations, and home market growth, more frequently caused younger than older businesses to sell products abroad. In contrast, old internationalized businesses more closely followed international business theories where the process was more deliberate, and firm factors predominated as motives. Host country distribution and transportation systems also were important to old businesses.

Research Question #4. What are the similarities and differences across young and old small businesses in their international strategies?

Entry mode did not differ significantly depending on age at internationalization. Ninety-seven percent engaged in exporting rather than licensing or foreign direct investment, although young businesses were more likely to export directly while old businesses exported indirectly. The international strategies differed by age as well. Young businesses exported a greater percent of total products, had a greater percent of total sales from exporting, and sold to a greater number of countries than old businesses. This implies early internationalization is associated with a "riskier" strategy characterized by a greater commitment to product sales and broader market scope. This behavior can be characterized as "entrepreneurial", and suggests motives explaining internationalization can be explained entrepreneurial theory. In contrast, late internationalization seems to follow administrative behavior, characterized by closer and fewer markets, and a lower percentage of product sales.

In all, this research reflected that small businesses do differ by age in their motives and international strategies. Further, these findings imply that age is more important in distinguishing between entrepreneurial and administrative behaviors than size (See Chapter I.) However, unsolicited orders and customer demand played a big role in the decision for both old and young businesses. The next section discusses the major conclusions and implications of this research.

CONCLUSIONS AND IMPLICATIONS

There are three main conclusions to this research, each having implications for researchers, managers, and public policy-makers. These three conclusions are: (1) internationalization in small businesses is serendipitous; (2) motives for internationalization vary by age; and (3) age at internationalization is associated with different strategies. Each will be discussed below.

(1) Internationalization in Small Businesses is Serendipitous.

The assumptions of theories of international business imply that internationalization is risky for small and young companies. As such, a conservative approach would be expected, where motives would be related to specific unique advantages or desire to resolve problems. Instead, thirty percent of the sample responded to unsolicited orders. Further, these companies engagement in international activities did not appear to be the result of long range planning. The overwhelming majority of these companies did not have a written plan to internationalize and noted that they didn't chose the country, but rather the customer from a particular country selected them. These businesses were responding to an opportunity or perceived product demand. This suggests opportunities for theory development. For researchers, a new mid-range theory may better explain motives for internationalization in small companies. A starting point for this integration is the role of "opportunity". Entrepreneurship literature presumes the perception and existence of an opportunity is a pre-condition for the creation of a venture (Timmons, 1985; Liebenstein, 1968). Similarly the behavioral stream of international business recognizes the perception of external opportunities abroad (Reid, 1980; Aharoni, 1966) will motivate internationalization. The presence of this concept in both domains suggests this concept may serve to link these two streams and offer a means to explain aspects of international entrepreneurship.

Another area of focus for researchers is the evidence that internationalization is not planned, sequential or even intentional. This supports theoretical arguments of Welch & Loustarinen (1988) and Melin (1992) who contest behavioral theories (stage models) are too deterministic. This view is similar to Gartner, Bird and Starr's (1992) description of emergent organizations where they suggested the creation is an enactment process, or socially constructed reality (Berger and Luckman, 1979). Similarly, Stone and Brush (1994) propose that planning in entrepreneurial firms can be interpretive rather than formal. Interpretive planning focuses on building commitment and attaining legitimacy. Interpretive planning is improvised and simultaneous, rather than analytical and sequential. Findings from this study imply there is an "enacted reality" aspect to the initial decision to sell abroad, while the subsequent planning is interpretive rather than formalized.

This research indicates that Oviatt and McDougall's (1994) definition of international new ventures may need to be expanded. Their work followed the economics stream arguing that seeking competitive advantage was a primary objective for these companies. The young companies in this study offered reasons besides competitive advantage, for instance; developing new markets, seeking relationships, and seeking sales abroad. Hence international new ventures, or companies internationalizing young in life may have a different motives. Clearly these findings imply additional exploration, and Oviatt and McDougall's conceptual work needs empirical testing. The following questions would be logical extensions of this research:

. What is the decision process used by owner/manager's in internationalizing their businesses? Does this differ depending on whether or not the founder is still present?

. What is the role of planning in internationalization, and how is it related to existing planning motives?

. What are the objectives sought by internationalized new companies? What are the relationships between these and company performance?

. Are the causes of internationalization similar or different for small service businesses and small product manufacturers?

. What motivates some businesses to take advantage of unsolicited opportunities and others not to do so?

The implication to small business managers is that they should scan the environment and be alert to opportunities (Aguilar, 1967). Technology is widely available for obtaining information about foreign markets, distribution channels, customers and suppliers. Moreover, visibility of company's unique product features and capabilities would appear to be important for attracting the attention of potential international customers. Instead of extensive time spent in formal business planning and market analysis, small companies should focus on public relations, advertising or networking through personal contacts abroad to encourage customers to inquire about products. Similarly, teachers should endeavor to help students learn scanning techniques, be knowledgeable about sources and types of information about possible international customers. Networking and communications skills are also essential.

For public policy makers, this conclusion suggests that the development of communication networks, or clearing houses where potential exporters, importers, buyers and suppliers can make contact with each other would be important. None of the small businesses indicated that they were motivated to export as a result of government incentives, contacts or information. Furthermore, conversations with small business owner/managers indicated that they found the information provided by both state and federal government sources to be "not too helpful"; they were better off "faxing or calling someone they knew overseas". On the other hand, the Federal Government provides a number or programs, in fact *Business Week*, April 6, 1992 points out more than eighteen federal agencies were involved in export promotions while twenty-three state governments were spending $50 million a year supporting technology extension centers. This suggests that resources being allocated to assist small businesses may need to be redirected. In other words, more effective programs that help small companies get in touch with future customers, suppliers or distributors abroad are needed. Similarly, several noted that U.S. "government red tape" was an obstacle, suggesting paperwork should be simplified to facilitate the internationalization process.

(2) Motives Differ by Age at Internationalization.
This study showed that age does matter when considering motives for internationalization in small companies. Motives for internationalization and strategies differed by age. The correlations and discriminant analysis were significant but weak. The major differences noted were that businesses selling products abroad at a young age were more frequently motivated by the contacts and expertise of management, the innovation of the product, and demand from the host country. In contrast, old businesses were catalyzed by planning, profits from domestic sales, experience, and trained employees. These characteristics are depicted below in Exhibit #7.1.

These results have implications for theory. First, these motives vary by company age at internationalization consistent with differences noted by the life cycle literature (see Chapter I). It was expected that younger companies would have a more dominant role of the founder, less formal systems and structure, and different goals than established businesses. These findings imply that stage of life cycle (using age as a surrogate) is more useful for explaining potential variations in international behaviors than size.

This research carefully examined size effects as a possible alternative explanation in motives for internationalization. Even though these firms were all small, (less than 100 employees) they were not of equal size in sales and revenues. However the lack of significance of size as an explanation for differences across business in reasons for internationalization has important implications for entrepreneurship researcher. In other words, age matters more than size as it relates to strategies of small firms. Similarly, researchers in international marketing have obtained many inconclusive results on the effect of size in exporting behavior. This research found that age explained more about internationalization than size. Hence age may be an important variable to focus on when trying

Exhibit #7.1

SUMMARY OF DIFFERENCES BETWEEN BUSINESSES YOUNG AND OLD AT INTERNATIONALIZATION

	Young	*Old*
management:	contacts (friends) skills expertise (finance & marketing)	
resources:	foreign market information employees with int'l experience	trained employees experience in domestic markets profits & sales
structure/ systems:	flexible operations	planning systems
competitive advantage:	innovative product ability to adapt to market changes	
strategy:	broad—several countries high percent of products high percent of sales	long term commitment employees abroad

to explain differential international behaviors or performance in small companies. Further comparisons of age and size in small business strategies and international strategies is an area suggested for further research.

Another point of interest for researchers is the nature of distinct differences. For young companies, the fact that contacts were catalysts differs from findings that planning and past experience were more prevalent in established companies. The factors affecting old companies support ideas from the stage theory of internationalization. However for young companies, there is little organizational experiential learning. It is possible that contacts, networks and business associates compensate for the organizational learning. The owner/manager has experience that can be transferred to the new company.

- What are the differences in the cognitive processes for managers of young versus old businesses in the decision to internationalize?

- What is the effect of experiential versus objective learning in the development of international strategy?

- What are the similarities/differences in international strategy content and process?

- Do small manufacturers from other countries have the same motives and strategies noted in this sample?

Exhibit #7.2 reflects a revised version of the conceptual framework used as a basis for this research. This revised framework includes variables found important in this research from theories of international business and entrepreneurship. While further adaptations of this descriptive framework may be made with future empirical testing, this framework recognizes the relatively greater importance of management factors and opportunity which were not included in the original conceptualization (See Exhibit #4.1).

The implications for small business managers are that international strategy does not have to be considered separate and later than start-up strategy. The start-up strategy of a new business can be international in scope. Experience in the marketplace is not necessary, but the personal experience, contacts and travel background of the owner/manager can be

Exhibit #7.2

REVISED CONCEPTUAL FRAMEWORK

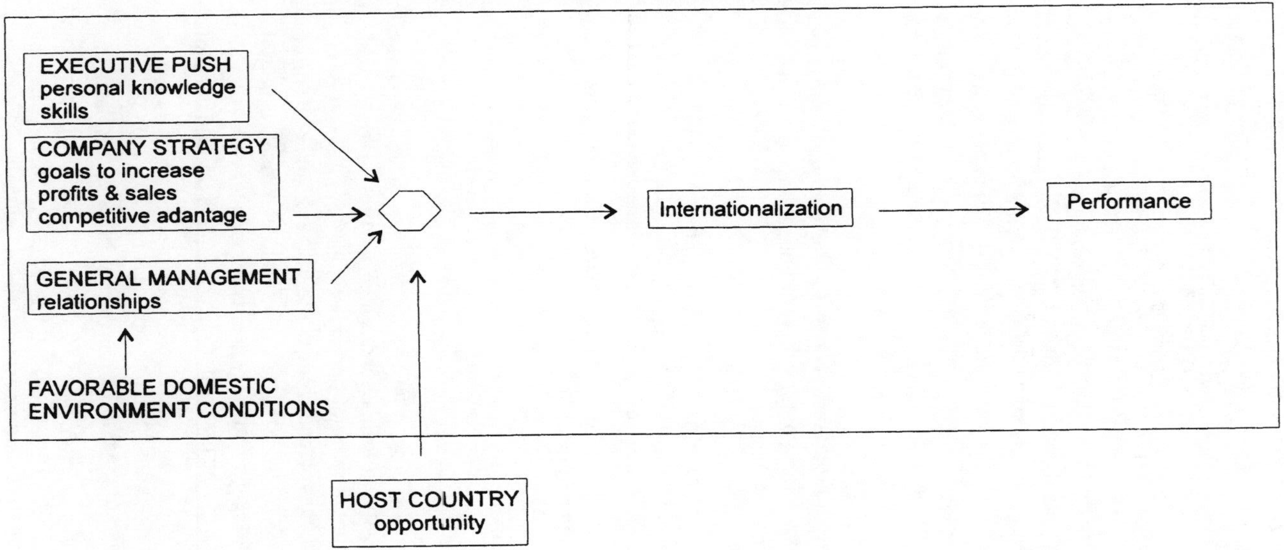

Performance

Internationalization

HOST COUNTRY
opportunity

EXECUTIVE PUSH
personal knowledge
skills

COMPANY STRATEGY
goals to increase
profits & sales
competitive adantage

GENERAL MANAGEMENT
relationships

FAVORABLE DOMESTIC
ENVIRONMENT CONDITIONS

helpful. However, given the obstacles noted by all businesses, persistence is an important ingredient in implementation. For teaching, this research points out that contrary to theories and available government data, businesses are internationalizing from start-up. Teaching cases about these companies illustrating how international product sales can be a part of initial start-up strategy similarly would be of great value.

Implications for public policy-makers suggest that businesses of different ages will have different needs in terms of information required and training. Blanket policies and programs for small business internationalization may need to be revised to recognize the different characteristics and strategies of small companies based on age.

(3)Age at Internationalization is Associated with Different Strategies.

This research found that not only did age affect motives, but also international strategies. There was evidence that early internationalization was associated with "riskier" strategies in that scope and commitment were broader and deeper than established businesses. This contradicts the stage theory which argues an incremental approach will permit the organization to decrease risk. The fact that nearly fifty percent of this sample internationalized within their first five years implies a revision to the stage model is needed (Melin, 1990). The stage model of internationalization is supported only for established businesses and not for young businesses. This is not to say that the stage model is wrong, rather there are examples of businesses "leap frogging", or skipping steps. Steps in the stage model may need to be revised to incorporate an accelerated stage "O" where activities occur simultaneously (pre-export–export) and transference of previous experiences of the management team are included.

On the other hand, this behavior or a riskier approach is consistent with entrepreneurial theory. Early internationalization implies that the decision to start-up may not be separate from the decision to internationalize. This is similar to work by Oviatt & McDougall (1994). For researchers, it will be important to investigate the nature of the start-up decision to determine in which instances internationalization is integrated or not.

The risky approach of young companies is another area of interest. Despite the fact that young companies often sold a high percentage of products to distant countries early in life, there was no significant performance disadvantage. Contrary to speculation, businesses selling abroad early did not perform more poorly than those that waited. There were no significant relationships between performance and age of internationalization. These findings indicate areas for future research:

. What factors from international business theories will explain better or worse performance of internationalized small businesses?

. What is the role of industry in determining international strategy?

. What strategy factors affect performance in internationalized small companies?

For managers, the implication is that early internationalization on a broad and deep scale can lead to performance equal to companies that do so later. Waiting can lead to missed opportunities, and a more conservative strategy. Hence, managers intending to sell abroad early should invest time in building relationships, developing innovative products, and structuring companies that are able to adapt to market changes rapidly. On the other hand, managers planning to internationalize late should spend time in investigating implementation strategies.

For public policy-makers, this conclusion suggests that government assistance, training, and information must be directed at both young and old businesses. Workshops and assistance programs for new venture creation should also include information about options for entering foreign markets. Incentives to encourage small firms to internationalize would also be appropriate. These small businesses continue to expand abroad and are important to the U.S. balance of trade.

FUTURE DIRECTIONS FOR INTERNATIONAL ENTREPRENEURSHIP

The international marketplace has changed. Innovations in telecommunications, transportation, information and computer technology have made it easier for small companies to be contacted by international customers and to promote and distribute their products worldwide. Public policy support, newly opened markets in Eastern Europe and Asia, and the implementation of global trade agreements have created a climate more favorable to small companies than ever before. As a consequence, the number of small businesses selling products abroad is steadily increasing. No longer is the international marketplace primarily the domain of large businesses.

These environmental changes, highlight the need to re-examine theories that explain behavior of businesses internationally. This research has probed the motives encouraging small businesses to sell abroad and considered the effect of age. The findings show that many businesses are selling abroad at an early age. While the motives of young and old businesses do differ, their performance does not. More importantly, the process of internationalization is very much the response to an opportunity, a concept that intersects both international business and entrepreneurship theory. Furthermore, variables from both entrepreneurship and international business were found to be important in explaining motives for selling abroad. The identification and description of these variables should spur further theory integration that will help to explain the behavior of small business as their role in the international marketplace changes.

As noted in the Introduction to this book, this research provides exploratory information about the domain of international entrepreneurship. This research focuses on the intersection of two fields where definitions are presently ill-defined, but interest is growing (Giamartino, McDougall, & Bird, 1993). Lack of consensus on definitions is characteristic of new domains of research. Narrowly conceived, the field of International Business states the focus is on the "the strategic behavior of firms competing in global markets in a world of nation-states" (Root, 1993). Clearly this definition argues for a focus on the "firm" as the unit of analysis, "multiple countries" as a context. On the other hand, entrepreneurship focuses on "new organizations pursuing opportunities" (Bygrave, 1989) and includes the individual, organization and networks as a unit of analysis. Entrepreneurial definitions do not specify context. For researchers intending to work at this intersection of two fields, it is important to look for areas of integration and synthesis. The Introduction of this book used a continuum of behaviors from administrative to entrepreneurial (Stevenson & Gumpert, 1984), and scope of operations from domestic to international as a means to establish boundaries to the domain of international entrepreneurship (See Exhibit I.1). The results of this study showed that there was a range of levels of involvement for internationalized companies. By considering only the international scope, an elaboration on this figure is possible. (See Exhibit #7.3.)

Exhibit #7.3

DOMAIN OF INTERNATIONAL
ENTREPRENEURSHIP - REVISED

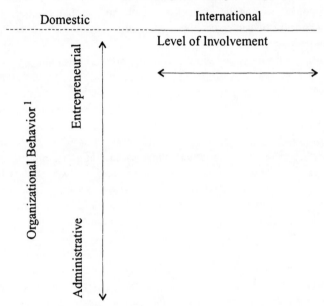

Geographical Scope of Operations

Domestic   International

Level of Involvement

Organizational Behavior[1]

Entrepreneurial

Administrative

[1]This continuum of behavior was proposed
by Stevenson & Gumpert (1985)

This revised exhibit allows for a range of levels of involvement internationally. Consistent with the findings of this research, companies may have greater or lesser commitment in terms of resources, people or markets. From this, a clearer articulation of types of future research is possible. For instance, a study of direct investment of new corporate ventures may arguably have a greater level of international involvement if it was to export. On the other hand, a multinational is likely more "administrative" in behavior than entrepreneurial. Depending on a researcher's definition and operationalization, one might see how a particular study falls into this new research domain.

As anecdotal evidence suggests, the boundaries between entrepreneurship and international business are becoming less clear. While the distinctions between domestic and international may be quite clear in the U.S., in other countries such as Denmark, Japan, and some Western European countries, these characteristics are less clear, and often unimportant. This research was intended to contribute to knowledge about the intersection of these two fields, to present information about a previously un-studied phenomenon. In some small way, I hope I have added a piece to this enormous puzzle we call entrepreneurship.

Appendix A

EMPIRICAL STUDIES FROM INTERNATIONAL BUSINESS

Abdel-Malek, 1978

Study tested differences in export orientation of large and small firms. Interviewed 58 CEO's from exporting and non-exporting Canadian manufacturers with less than $20 million in sales. Findings- Few significant differences were found in export orientation by size of company.

Adams & Hall, 1993

Using data base from STRATOS project, this paper examines influences on performance in 1,132 SME companies (< 500 employees) from 8 European countries. Results show country specific, competitive and market factors affect export performance, while personal factors were relatively more important. Authors concluded that SME's were constrained by their environments.

Aharoni, 1966

Author investigated motives and process in foreign investment decision. Interviewed 27 companies with investments abroad. Findings- Strength of external threats/opportunities or internal impetus motivates FDI. Supported Cyert & March (1963) decision process except that role of leader, environment and innovation played greater roles.

Ali & Swiercz, 1991

Tested relationships between firm size, export experience and attitudes. Surveyed 195 companies having less than $5 million in sales. Findings- Size was not related to attitudes toward internationalization, but was related to perceptions and skills required for selling abroad.

Baird, Lyles & Orris, 1994

The choice of international strategies in small companies (< 500 employees) was studied in this 160 mixed industry U.S. companies. Findings-internationalized companies were larger, manufacturers, and often did not plan formally. International strategy was positively related to ROS but negatively related to growth.

Beamish & Munro, 1986

Export motivations and performance were studied in this sample of 116 small Canadian companies. More than 30% were motivated by unsolicited orders, the majority exporting to the U.S. Correlations showed that profit was related to large size, product modifications and customer service.

Bilkey & Tesar, 1977

Study tested stage model of internationalization. Surveyed 423 small and medium-sized Wisconsin manufacturers. Findings-Unsolicited orders motivated exporting; the stage model was supported.

Bilkey, 1978

Purpose was to research factors distinguishing between exporters and non-exporters. Surveyed 423 small and medium-sized Wisconsin manufacturers, some exporters and some non-exporters. Findings- Manager's experience, foreign language ability, travel, view of risk, cultural similarity, available capital and information motivated exporting.

Bijmolt & Zwart, 1994

Adapting a framework from Aaby & Slater, factors leading to export performance were studied. 248 small businesses (< 200 employees) from the Netherlands were cluster analyzed, forming four distinct groups. Conclusions-firm characteristics (size, business plan, years experience) affected strategy (product, technology). Performance was related to efforts to improve export performance (planning and use of policy instruments).

Calof, 1993

This data base study of Canadian businesses investigated the relationship between size and internationalization. Findings showed that size (using a sales measure) did not limit ability to export, larger companies were more profitable, size was not related to export intensity, and that the number of countries was related to larger sized companies.

Cavusgil, 1979

Investigated factors distinguishing between exporters and non-exporters. Surveyed 423 small and medium-sized manufacturers, some exporters and some non-exporters. Findings- Favorable attitude of management was important motive.

Cavusgil & Nevin, 1981

Study researched firm determinants of export behavior. Surveyed 423 small and medium-sized Wisconsin manufacturers, some exporters and some non-exporters. Findings- Differences in export behavior were due to characteristics of firm, and management commitment and interest.

Cavusgil, 1982

Purpose was to investigate factors distinguishing between stages of exporting. Surveyed manufacturing firms in Maine and New Mexico by mail survey to CEO's. Findings- Management commitment affected stages, manager's experience was related to growth, size was not important.

Cavusgil, 1984

Study investigated differences among export firms across stages in exporting. Interviewed 70 CEO's from manufacturers in Wisconsin and Illinois. Findings- Life cycle stage is related to market research internationally; level of sales and profits did not differentiate among stages.

Cavusgil & Naor, 1987

Explored firm and management characteristics important to export behavior. Surveyed 310 firms in Maine, exporters and non-exporters. Findings- Manager's experience in finance and planning, higher level of education, product characteristics, access to distribution and available foreign market information differentiated between exporters and non-exporters.

Chatterjee, 1990

Investigated factors determining market entry by direct investment or acquisition. Data base analysis of 47 Fortune 500 companies. Findings- Concentration of markets and high stock prices related to acquisition; availability of internal funds was related to direct investment.

Christensen, daRocha & Gertner, 1987

Researched factors determining export success in exporters and non-exporters. Sample composed of 152 Brazilian manufacturers. Findings- Greater quality control, size and diversification associated with exporters.

Clegg, 1990

Study investigated industry and country determinants of international non-affiliate licensing. Data base analysis of manufacturers from 5 countries. Findings- Country specific differences lead to different models (strategies) for licensing.

Contractor, 1985

Research investigated why companies engage in international licensing rather than foreign direct investment as corporate strategy. Analyzed Department of Commerce data base composed of 241 companies. Findings- Licensing is a profitable alternative to foreign direct investment; constraints on direct investment such as trade policy and international risk, or goals such as desire for fast market entry motivated licensing.

Cooper & Kleinschmidt, 1985

Authors studied the impact of export strategy on performance in small firms. Personal interviews with 142 Canadian firms having sales of less than $20 million. Findings- Types of market, segmentation strategies and product strategies contributed to performance (exporting sales to total sales). Firm size and sales were not related. Market orientation and "world view" of management were related to better performance.

Czinkota & Johnston, 1981

Study attempted to differentiate firms based on level of international activities. Surveyed 237 small and medium sized materials manufacturers. Findings- Stages of internationalization differentiates firms better than size, service or managerial attitude.

Dominguez & Sequeira, 1993

Strategic decision-making and firm characteristics in export performance were examined in a cross-national survey of 279 Central American companies. Based on Aaby & Slater (1989), results showed high sales were related to high volume/high growth strategies; low cost/high volume strategies experienced lower sales; and low volume/ undifferentiated strategieses resulted in marginal performance.

D'Souza & Eramilli, 1990

Investigated the motives and choices for foreign market entry in small service firms. Surveyed 175 computer consulting and technical services firms, (< $5 million in sales). Findings- response to client request, top market choice was preference for English speaking country motived foreign market entry.

Eramilli & Rao, 1990

Variations in entry mode choice in service companies was studied in 173 U.S. companies. Findings: client following and market seeking distinctions can be made, but relationships between market knowledge and entry mode were not supported.

Galbraith, DeNoble & Estavillo, 1990

Researched the location criteria and perceptions of business climate in Mexico in small U.S. companies. Sample composed of 55 electronics assemblies firms in Baja California, and 45 U.S. based electronics firms. Findings- Perceptions of business climate specifically low cost labor, stable political environment and infrastructure were important in the location decision.

Geringer, Beamish & daCosta, 1989

Study explored performance differences in MNE's. Analyzed diversification strategies of 100 largest MNE's. Findings- Related diversification strategy is associated with better performance.

Gomez-Casseres & Kohn, 1990

Authors studied how small firms (<1000 employees) compete using technology internationally. Sample was 1200 U.S. high technology companies with extensive direct investment abroad. Findings- Small firms compete using deep niche, narrow market strategy. Dominant position and large size are not requirement for success in high technology companies abroad.

Goodnow & Hansz, 1972

Investigated environmental determinants on market entry strategy. Analyzed data base of characteristics of 100 countries and surveys from 222 firms. Findings- Availability of information and positive environmental factors (political, government, legal, physio-graphic, geo-cultural) encourage exporting, joint ventures or foreign investment.

Green & Cunningham, 1975

Research studied extent to which factors determining foreign investment supported Aharoni's (1966) work. Analyzed data base of U.S. companies having foreign direct investment in 25 countries. Findings- Total allocation of foreign investment related to country GNP, population and expected profit. Marketing potential determined foreign investment.

Gripsrud, 1989

Explored determinants decisions of Norwegian firms to export to distant markets. Sample composed of 131 fishery process companies in Norway. Findings- Larger companies more likely to export to markets a greater distance away; product categories important. Experience influences attitude toward future expectations.

Hirsch & Adar, 1974

Analyzed effect of firm size on export performance. Method involved data base test of model. Findings- Results showed strong relationship between export performance and firm size in several industries.

Hisrich & Peters, 1983

Study explored participation and attitude of U.S. manufacturers in East-West trade. Mail survey of 140 large U.S. manufactures; 50 involved in East-West trade. Findings- Motive for trade was desire to have long term access to markets. Government support and political climate had little effect on attitude toward East-West trade.

Holzmuller & Kasper, 1990

Investigated the effect of decision-maker orientation on export activities. Surveyed 103 Austrian companies by mail. Findings- Firm orientation is important in exporting, even though measurement of "orientation" is difficult due to cultural dimensions.

Holzmuller & Kasper, 1991

Based on a study of 116 Austrian firms, this study develops a causal analytic model of exporting. Authors show that cognitive (know how, knowledge) are supplemented by non-cognitive (attitudes, values, norms) in the decision to export.

Horst, 1972

Researched factors affecting the decision of multinationals to go abroad. Analyzed a data base using a model. Findings- Size (market share) was a significant factor in the business' decision to invest abroad.

Johnston & Czinkota, 1982

Authors investigated factors discriminating between exporters and non-exporters. Cross-sectional survey of national sample of 181 consumer goods companies. Findings- Exporting is result of proactive and reactive motives. Major motives were profit, unique product, technology advantage, management urge, tax benefits, competitive pressures and market advantage. Proactive-had greater service, sales volume and broader strategy; reactive-focused on operations.

Kaynak, 1992

Regional differences in motives to export between 104 "prairie" and 92 "Atlantic" firms were investigated. Findings showed causes of exporting were desire to use excess capacity, unsolicited orders, desire to make a high profit, and belief in niche for products. Regional differences existed between managers' insights and information, and use of assistance. Regional variations in products also were present.

Kedia & Chokar, 1985

Purpose was to investigate the importance of managers perceptions of costs and risks in exporting. Interviewed 49 exporters, 47 non-exporters in food processing industry from Louisiana. Findings- Negative attitude of manager is barrier to exporting; non-exporters perceive costs differently. Profiles of managers from exporting and non-exporting companies differed.

Kirplani & MacIntosh, 1980

Investigated factors affecting international marketing effectiveness of technology-oriented small firms. Sample composed of 34 high technology firms; 10 from the U.S. and 24 from Canada having less than 1000 employees. Findings- Age of company (younger) related to greater success in terms of growth in total sales, and growth in export sales. Price, promotion and technology leadership also associated with better performance.

Kobrin, 1991

Analyzed industry structure determinants of global integration. Employed data base analysis to test model. Findings- Scale economies were less important than technology intensity in decision to integrate globally.

Kohn, 1988

Study investigated foreign direct investment by small U.S. based manufacturers. Analyzed Dept. of Commerce data base. Findings- Costs, strategy and technology advantage were important in the decision to invest abroad.

Kothari, 1978

Researched strategic exporting approaches of U.S. manufactures in international markets. Sample composed of 308 Texas manufacturers with less than 250 employees. Findings- Competition at home, limited domestic opportunity and unique skills and knowledge motive exporting.

Kwei Chong & Wai Chong, 1988

Study explored differences between small and medium sized exporting firms. Sample composed of Korean furniture manufacturers having less than 150 employees. Findings- Exporters with more employees perceived more marketing strength abroad.

Langston & Teas, 1976

Authors researched differences between exporting and non-exporting firms. Findings- Companies are more likely to export when managers have lived and travelled abroad.

Lecraw, 1983

Research investigated determinants of performance in transnational manufacturers. Surveyed 153 managers of subsidiaries of 5 ASEAN countries; all were light manufacturers. Findings- Competitive advantage of transnational companies are different in domestic markets than internationally.

Lecraw, 1984

Study explored the degree of importance of structural and firm characteristics on diversification strategy and performance. Sample included 200 publicly held non-financial firms from Canada. Findings- Determinants analysis showed that choice of base industry and firm characteristics influenced diversification strategy.

Lecraw, 1989

Investigated factors influencing success in counter-trade. Mail survey of 152 exporters from U.S., Japan and Canada was conducted. Findings- Large firms with experience in exporting and counter-trade, with high value, highly visible complex products were better able to succeed in counter trade. Supports economic theory where success in counter-trade is related to larger size.

Lim, Sharkey & Kim, 1991

This study developed a Lisrel model, using the innovation adoption process as a basis for characterizing the export adoption process. Using a sample of 438 Ohio manufacturers, direct effects showed strong relationships between interest and intention, and weak effects between awareness and interest, and intention and adoption.

Lindquist, 1990

Research investigated international success in exporting of small Swedish firms. Conducted survey of 85 Swedish companies by mail. Findings- Level of commitment to foreign markets was related to success; more resources committed and positive attitude of management, the better the performance.

Liouville, 1992

A sample of 137 W. German mechanical engineering firms was studied to explore the conditions under which exporting would lead to higher profits. Findings showed size was not significant, in that larger companies did not benefit from exporting more than smaller companies. Factors leading to profit included recession and less competition. Specialization of business was not significant.

Lorange & Roos, 1990

Study investigated differences in managerial approaches to cooperative venture formation in 67 Norwegian and Swedish industrial firms, forming 33 pairs of cooperative ventures. Authors found distinct differences in overall strategies. Swedish firms tended to have expansion as a goal and be motivated by internal entrepreneurial forces; whereas Norwegian companies sought compatible partners, were motivated by intuition, and did not approach the decision analytically.

Malezadeh & Nahavandi, 1985

Purpose was to investigate the impact of competitive advantage on the motivation to export or not to export. Surveyed 296

California exporting and non-exporting manufacturers. Findings- Exporters and non-exporters differ based on how they plan for new markets. Determinants in decision to export included taxes and proximity to foreign markets.

McDougall, 1989

Researched differences in strategy and structure of new ventures having domestic and international operations. Sample composed of 269 Dun and Bradstreet listed businesses of less than 8 years old. Findings- Strategy and structure variables differed between domestic and international operations; most distinguishing in computer, and communications industry. Domestic businesses emphasized product expansion strategy while international businesses emphasized greater distribution, competitive and market strategies.

Millington & Bayliss, 1990

Study tested sequential model of internationalization. Sample composed of 50 manufacturing companies in the United Kingdom. Findings- Results did not support the stepwise internationalization model. Planning was important in joint ventures.

Namiki, 1988

Study examined types of export strategies in small firms. Sample composed of 3 computer hardware companies having less than 250 employees. Findings- Small firms differentiated by marketing, innovation, and product quality. Multiple strategies used for competing internationally. Higher performing firms followed a single strategy.

O'Rourke, 1985

Explored differences in attitude, practices and problems in exporters by size of business. Surveyed by mail 304 companies from the Northwestern U.S. Findings- Skilled personnel, smaller (in sales) more often responded to unsolicited orders or contacts. Government contacts not a factor. Larger firms were more proactive in initiating exporting.

Pak & Weaver, 1990

Investigated differences among exporters based on level of involvement (extent to which depended on export activity). Conducted national survey of 566 small exporters. Findings-International experience of top management (spoke foreign language, lived abroad) related to interest in growth abroad. Age was not related to export involvement.

Piercy, 1981

This study explored active and reactive behaviors in 250 English SME manufacturers. Results showed that active and reactive can be distinguished, active being large, having greater sales volume, more profitable and small being smaller, having lower sales volume and offering a more specialized product.

Pinney, 1970

Research investigated the importance of top management attitudes in exporting. Surveyed 209 manufacturers from Indiana. Findings- Firms with younger age and managers with positive attitude toward internationalization are more likely to export.

Rabino, 1980

Study investigated barriers to exporting faced by small firms. Sample composed of 46 Massachusetts companies, 17 were high technology firms. Findings- Advantages of exporting perceived to be increased sales, and diversification; biggest barrier was distribution abroad.

Reid, 1984

Purpose was to investigate information acquisition and intent to export in small firms. Sample composed of 89 Canadian fabricated metal (furniture) manufacturers (71 exporters and 18 non-exporters). Findings-Multiple sources of information associated greater expansion; low usage of government programs.

Roy & Simpson, 1981

Researched CEO perceptions of costs and profits in export marketing. Sample composed of 124 companies with less than

500 employees; 65 were exporters. Findings- CEOs in smaller firms perceive more risk in exporting; no significant differences between exporters and non-exporters except that exporters perceived greater costs and profits.

Samuels, Greenfield & Mpuku, 1992

This study explored pricing behavior and attitude toward risk in 60 SME's from England. Results showed a significant correlation between length of time in exporting and size, as well as a reluctance of small companies to alter prices when international exchange rates fluctuated.

Simpson & Kujawa, 1974

Studied factors distinguishing between exporters and non-exporters. Sample composed of 120 Tennessee manufacturers (50 exporters and 70 non-exporters). Findings- Unsolicited orders, high level of manager education, low perceived risk, available resources (management time, money, personnel & information), and low perceived costs associated with exporters.

Singer & Czinkota, 1992

Study examines factors associated with effective use of export assistance. Sample was composed of 89 small (< 500 employees) that had solicited assistance form the Minnesota Office of Trade. Results found no relationship between assistance used and export state, but the relationship between management commitment and assistance was positive.

Sriram & Sapienza, 1991

Role of marketing variables associated with export involvement was studied in sample of marketing executives in 121 exporting firms. Findings- Small (< 250 employees) and large companies vary in marketing activities; large focus on individual buyers and export to more countries than small.

Sullivan & Bauerschmidt, 1990

Research tested stage model of internationalization, barriers and incentives to exporting. Surveyed 62 forest products companies from Austria, Finland, Sweden and West Germany by mail. Findings-Internationalization is a strategic decision that must fit into cognitive and resource character of the company. Manager's perceptions of foreign markets and country conditions motivate entry.

Sweeney, 1970

Investigated factors important in successful internationalization of small companies. Case study methodology was employed. Findings-Commitment and communication were found vital to success.

Telesio, 1979

Study investigated decision to license technology abroad. Sample composed of 200 managers of Fortune 500 companies. Findings- Motives for licensing were desire to supplement resources and reciprocate exchanges; companies with high percent research and development, large size, experience internationally, and high level of diversification more likely to consider licensing.

Tesar, 1977

Explored planning. attitudes and operational differences in exporters and non-exporters. Sample composed of 423 small and medium-sized manufacturers in Wisconsin. Findings- Proximity to market encouraged exporting; product characteristics, technology advantage, and greater sales volume associated with exporting.

Tookey, 1964

Examined differences between exporters and on-exporters. Sample composed of 54 clothing manufacturers from Great Britain. Findings- Larger firms with experienced managers more likely to export; lack of trained staff can be a handicap in exporting.

Tyebjee, 1990

Investigated factors causing high technology ventures to internationalize. Surveyed 105 high technology start-up in 8 industries. Findings- Factors motivating international involvement and international success are different; firm demographics are motives for selling abroad while management activities and product adaptations are related to success. Larger size firms are more likely to internationalize.

Ursic & Czinkota, 1984

Study investigated the effect of experience curve on propensity to export. Surveyed 126 companies (100 old; 26 young) U.S. exporters in 3 industries. Findings- Younger aged firms had more favorable attitude toward exporting than older.

Vachani, 1989

Study examined the effect of country environment on MNE diversification. Employed data base analysis of overseas subsidiaries of Fortune 500 MNE's. Findings- There is less incidence of foreign direct investment in lower developed countries; companies in these market use high advertising and low research and development. No significant differences in experiences and behaviors of subsidiaries across type of country.

Walters, 1993

Patterns of planning in U.S. firms and relationship to performance in 167 companies is investigated. Findings show most companies do not plan, and that size is related to more planning. Contrary to earlier research, those companies achieving the highest performance conducted only limited formal planning and gathered less information. Non-planners behaved intuitively. Only in very small firms was formal planning associated with sales growth.

Weidersheim-Paul, Olson & Welch, 1978

Investigated factors distinguishing between exporting and non-exporting firms. Developed model which was tested on data base. Findings- In manufacturing firms, unique assets and favorable orientation of management encourage exporting.

Welch & Weidersheim-Paul, 1980

Research investigated factors influencing decision to export. Developed model which was tested on data base. Findings- Older age of firm, receipt of unsolicited orders and perceived low psychic distance were motives for exporting.

Withey, 1980

Study investigated differences between small exporters and non-exporters. Sample composed of 357 small mid-western manufacturers having less than 500 employees; 166 were exporters. Findings- Larger businesses (more than 50 employees) were more likely to export. Exporters had more "global" perspective than non-exporters.

Yaprak, 1985

Investigated differences between small exporting and non-exporting firms. Sample composed of 84 exporters and 44 non-exporters from Michigan. Findings- Available resources, especially capital encouraged exporting.

Appendix B

DESCRIPTION OF PUBLISHED LISTS
FROM DIRECTORIES USED FOR SAMPLING

1. *Corporate Technology Directory* (1991), 6th U.S. Edition, Woburn, MA: Corporate Technology Information Services, Inc.

    Company profiles are provided in each listing. This directory lists address, phone number, establishment date, sales, employees, internationalization status, management team, SIC codes, and a brief description of the products sold.

2. *Dun's Principle International Businesses: World Marketing Directory* (1991) New York: Dun and Bradstreet

    This directory identifies companies by name, SIC code, number of employees, sales, CEO, address, telephone number, establishment date, and whether or not the company is internationalized (no differentiation is made between exporting of foreign direct investment). Approximately 7900 businesses are listed.

3   *Partner's in Export Trade, Directory for Export Trade Contacts* (1987), Volume 2, Washington, D.C.: U.S. Department of Commerce

    This directory lists about 4,500 U.S. based companies and products/services by state. Phone number, address, and CEO name are listed.

4. *Ward's Directory of U.S. Private and Public Companies* (1989-1990), Detroit, Michigan: Gale Research Inc.

    Approximately 90,000 companies are listed in this directory which provides information about products by SIC code, export involvement, categorical information on sales and employees, year of establishment, address, phone number and CEO name.

5   *U.S. Import/Export Directory*   (1990) Volume 2, New York: *Journal of Commerce*

The U.S. Import/Export Directory is published by the *Journal of Commerce* every year. About 17,300 exporting companies are listed. Companies are listed by state, and data includes products/services produced, SIC code, date of establishment, names of CEO and management team, number of countries served, percentage of sales from international markets, ports of exit, bank references, number of employees, FAX, telephone and address.

6. In addition to published lists, two listings from small business associations were made available to the researcher. The total number of companies surveyed in this sample was forty-nine. Eight of this small sample responded and these businesses were similar in every way to the rest of the companies responding. These two organizations will remain anonymous as per their request.

Appendix C-1

TOTAL EXPORT DOLLARS BY REGION
AND TOP COUNTRY OF EXPORT[1]

Region I	*Millions Dollars*	*Top Country*	*Top Country Percentage*
Connecticut $	3,828	Japan	18%
Massachusetts	9,691	Japan	14%
Maine	805	Canada	37%
New Hampshire	1,025	G.Britain	18%
Rhode Island	559	Canad	23%
Vermont	1,172	Canada	70%

Region II			
New Jersey	8,308	Canada	16%
New York	26,961	Canada	14%

Region III			
Delaware	1,202	Canada	75%
Washington D.C.	269	W. Germany	39%
Maryland	2,551	Canada	31%
Pennsylvania	7,801	Canada	25%
West Virginia	1,349	Canada	23%
Virginia	7,887	Belgium	16%

Region IV			
Alabama	2,867	Japan	20%
Florida	13,423	Venezuela	9%
Georgia	4,889	Canada	13%
Kentucky	2,938	Canada	26%
Mississippi	1,359	Canada	18%
North Carolina	6,786	Canada	17%
South Carolina	2,997	Canada	16%
Tennessee	2,995	Canada	27%

Region V	Millions Dollars	Top Country	Top Country Percentage
Illinois	11,513	Canada	27%
Indiana	4,758	Canada	38%
Michigan	21,015	Canada	71%
Minnesota	5,093	Canada	21%
Ohio	12,276	Canada	42%
Wisconsin	4,727	Canada	30%
Region VI			
Arkansas	709	Canada	32%
Louisiana	14,921	Canada	17%
New Mexico	193	Canada	12%
Oklahoma	1,541	Canada	31%
Texas	34,578	Mexico	27%
Region VII			
Iowa	2,164	Canada	35%
Kansas	1,961	Japan	16%
Missouri	2,737	Canada	30%
Nebraska	916	Japan	21%
Region VIII			
Colorado	2,098	Japan	20%
Montana	398	Japan	34%
North Dakota	279	Canada	53%
South Dakota	91	Canada	38%
Utah	943	Canada	22%
Wyoming	235	Canada	29%

Region IX

Arizona	3,547	Mexico	22%
California	47,789	Japan	18%
Hawaii	202	Japan	56%
Nevada	248	Switzerland	20%

Region X	*Millions Dollars*	*Top Country*	*Top Country Percentage*
Alaska	2,358	Japan	74%
Idaho	697	Japan	24%
Oregon	4,522	Japan	29%
Washington	17,865	Japan	27%

1- Source: U.S. Bureau of Census, Foreign Trade Division, University of Massachusetts, MISER Services, 1988

Appendix C-2

TOP FIVE INDUSTRIES OF EXPORT
IN 1983 AND 1987

1983   *SIC Code*

1. Electrical Machinery   35
2. Transportation Equipment   37
3. Chemicals & Allied Products   28
4. Electrical & Electronic   36
5. Primary Metals   33

— Source: Mehl, G. (1983)

1987   *SIC Code*

1. Transportation Equipment   37
2. Chemicals & Allied Products   28
3. Electrical & Electronic   36
4. Machinery except Electrical   35
5. Auxiliary Office Products   40

— Source: Office of Finance, Industry
   & Trade (1991)

Appendix C-3

NUMBER OF FOREIGN TRADE ZONES
AND PORTS BY REGION

Region I	*Number of Foreign Trade Zones[1]*	*Number of Ports [2]*
Connecticut	2	1
Massachusetts	2	2
Maine	1	1
New Hampshire	1	1
Rhode Island	1	1
Vermont	2	-
Region II		
New Jersey	2	5
New York	12	23
Region III		
Delaware	1	1
Washington, D.C.	1	1
Maryland	2	1
Pennsylvania	3	7
West Virginia	-	-
Virginia	2	2
Region IV		
Alabama	3	3
Florida	8	13
Georgia	2	8
Kentucky	2	3
Mississippi	1	6
North Carolina	4	5
South Carolina	3	5
Tennessee	3	2

	Number of Foreign Trade Zones[1]	*Number of Ports* [2]
Region V		
Illinois	3	17
Indiana	2	4
Michigan	4	2
Minnesota	2	3
Ohio	6	5
Wisconsin	1	4
Region VI		
Arizona	1	3
Louisiana	3	25
New Mexico	1	-
Oklahoma	2	2
Texas	16	14
Region VII		
Iowa	2	-
Kansas	1	-
Missouri	2	1
Nebraska	2	-
Region VIII		
Colorado	2	-
Montana	1	1
North Dakota	1	-
South Dakota	-	-
Utah	1	-
Wyoming	-	-

	Number of Foreign Trade Zones[1]	*Number of Ports* [2]
Region IX		
Arizona	4	-
California	4	13
Hawaii	1	1
Nevada	1	-
Region X		
Arkansas	1	3
Idaho	-	2
Oregon	2	10
Washington	8	19

[1] Source: Goldsmith, H. (1989) *Import/Export: A Guide to Profit and Market Share*, NY: Prentice Hall, pp. 177-196

[2] Source: *U.S. Import/Export Directory*, New York: *Journal of Commerce*, Inc. pp. 799-808

Appendix C-4

HIGHLIGHTS OF U.S. GOVERNMENT EXPORT PROMOTION ACTIVITIES 1982-1992[1]

1980-1985   34 states sponsored more than 300 export trade activi-
                   ties and trade fairs

1982-   Export Trading Company Act passed- joint export
                   initiatives allowed

1984-   19 states received federal funding for export promotion
                   activities   27 states ran more than 52 overseas trade
                   and investment offices in 10 countries

1987-   47 states sponsored organized trade missions
                   27 states ran over 80 overseas trade and investment
                   offices in 40 countries

1992-   18 federal agencies involved in export promotion
                   activities
                   23 state governments spend more than $50 million a
                   year supporting
                   27 technology extension centers

[1] Sources: Seringhaus, 1992; Penner, 1991

Appendix C-5

COUNTRIES ACCOUNTING FOR THE MOST GROWTH IN U.S. EXPORTS[1]

Country	1986- Billions $	1991- Billions $	Percent Increase
Canada	$ 55.0	$ 85.1	55%
Japan	26.6	48.1	80%
Mexico	12.4	33.3	168%
Germany	10.4	21.3	105%
G. Britain	11.3	22.1	95%
Korea	5.9	15.1	155%
France	7.2	15.4	114%
Taiwan	5.2	13.2	154%

1- Holstein, W.J. & Kelly, K.(1992) "Little Companies, Big Exports", *Business Week*, Apr. 13, 1992

Appendix D

Company A- This company was a producer of small electronic dermatology products founded in 1982, but first sold abroad at age four. Current sales were $10,000,000 and the company employed 50 people. In year one of exporting, the company sold products in England subsequent to the owner's travel experiences there. The owner, a chemist by training explained that his main reasons for internationalization were personal experiences abroad and knowledge of similar products sold in Europe. As he noted; "I KNEW there was a market abroad, and I never considered anything but international sales. Competing products required wires and plugs, whereas our product was battery operated and electrical conversion was not a problem". The process of internationalization for this company was gradual, personnel constraints made it necessary to sell abroad slowly. Biggest obstacles were cash flow and language, but barriers to entry were not important in the decision.

Company B- A California based manufacturer of microfiche products, this $9 million dollar company employs eighty people. Founded in 1974, the company sold abroad after eight years of operations. The founder noted the industry was internationalizing and in order to maintain relationships, it was important for her company to begin to sell products abroad. Similarly, customers and clients abroad had inquired about the product. Obtaining U.S. government approvals and endorsements facilitated entry into foreign markets. This company plans to license its products abroad soon.

Company C- This computer software manufacturer will reach 300 employees and $35 million in sales this year. The company was founded twelve years ago but first sold its products abroad at age five. The owner noted "I always envisioned my business as international from the start. I attended a graduate program about the time I was starting this business company didn't internationalize sooner". This owner felt that cultural aspects and education were not terribly important, rather customer demand was more important.

Company D- A manufacturer of golf clubs, this business started in 1987 and internationalized within the first year when a Japanese customer suggested they sell abroad. Approximately fourteen percent of the products are shipped abroad by an indirect exporter. The owner's vision was "world-wide" from the start. The present sales are about $800,000.

Company E- A southern based manufacturer of custom elevators, the owner stated the company had "no choice but to expand markets and step outside the U.S.". There was market demand abroad, whereas the big companies were competitive in domestic markets. This company internationalized at age five when sales were nearly four million. Problems have been encountered only in follow-up servicing.

Appendix E

Questionnaire

Boston University

Entrepreneurial Management Institute
School of Management
621 Commonwealth Avenue
Boston, Massachusetts 02215
617/353-4298

Office of the Director

October 15, 1991

Dear Entrepreneur:

The attached survey is **one of the first national studies** about the international business activities of small businesses. Although a growing number of small manufacturers are selling their products outside of the U.S., little is known about the international experiences of these companies. This project will provide information about opportunities, problems, and key factors to success for small businesses in the global marketplace. I am asking for your participation in this research.

This survey should take 20 minutes to complete. In return for your help, I will send you a copy of the summary results from this study. **Your responses will remain completely confidential** and no individual respondents or companies will be identified by name.

Your knowledge and experiences are very important to this project. Please submit your responses <u>before November 30, 1991</u>. Enclosed is a self-addressed postage paid envelope for your convenience. You may also FAX the completed survey to (617) 353-2564. Please include your business card if you would like to receive a copy of the summary results.

Thank you for your help and participation.

Very truly yours,

Candida G. M

Candida G. Brush
Doctoral Candidate and Project
    Director
Entrepreneurial Management Institute
(617) 353-4413

Enclosure

INTERNATIONAL BUSINESS QUESTIONNAIRE

This survey is part of a national study of small manufacturers and their international activities. This survey should be completed by a manager or owner who was with the firm when the business first sold its products abroad. You and your responses will remain COMPLETELY ANONYMOUS. The term "internationalized" means "PRODUCTS SOLD AND REVENUES RECEIVED FROM OUTSIDE THE U.S.". Thank you for your time.

1. In what YEAR:
   a. was your company ESTABLISHED? _____ (year)

   b. did your company FIRST DECIDE TO SELL ITS PRODUCTS ABROAD?____ (year)

   c. were your company's PRODUCTS FIRST SOLD ABROAD? _____ (year)

2. WHY did your company first DECIDE to SELL ITS PRODUCTS ABROAD? (Please list in order of importance the top three reasons.)

   1._____
   2._____
   3._____

3. WHAT was the FIRST FOREIGN COUNTRY(s) in which your products were sold?
   _____

   a. WHY did your company SELECT this particular COUNTRY(s)?_____
      _____

   b. WHAT was your company's ORIGINAL MEANS OF ENTRY into this COUNTRY'S markets? (Please check one.)

   direct export   __   franchising
   indirect export through intermediary __   licensing   __
   sole venture direct investment   __   contracting   __
   joint venture direct investment   __
   other: (please specify)_____

4. The following questions relate to PRODUCTS SOLD ABROAD in YEAR #1 of product sales abroad and TODAY.

	Year #1 of Sales Abroad	Today
a. MAIN PRODUCTS sold abroad	_____	_____
	_____	_____
b. TOTAL NUMBER of COUNTRIES where product was sold	_____	_____
c. PERCENTAGE of TOTAL MANU- FACTURED PRODUCTS sold abroad	_____ %	_____ %

5. Did your business have a WRITTEN LONG RANGE PLAN for international expansion when your company first sold its product abroad? Yes ___ No___

1

6. What has been the BIGGEST OBSTACLE(S) faced in the INTERNATIONALIZATION PROCESS?

_____
_____
_____

7. Please rate your opinion of the FAVORABILITY of the BUSINESS CONDITIONS FOR YOUR COMPANY in the U.S. in YEAR #1 of sales abroad and TODAY. Please circle the number that applies. (DK= don't know)

	U.S. Conditions in Year #1		U.S. Conditions Today	
	not favorable	favorable	not favorable	favorable
Economic conditions	DK 1 2 3 4 5		DK 1 2 3 4 5	
Tax laws	DK 1 2 3 4 5		DK 1 2 3 4 5	
Trade regulations	DK 1 2 3 4 5		DK 1 2 3 4 5	
Foreign market information	DK 1 2 3 4 5		DK 1 2 3 4 5	
Capital resources	DK 1 2 3 4 5		DK 1 2 3 4 5	
Experienced employees	DK 1 2 3 4 5		DK 1 2 3 4 5	
Raw materials and supplies	DK 1 2 3 4 5		DK 1 2 3 4 5	
Customer demand	DK 1 2 3 4 5		DK 1 2 3 4 5	
Market size	DK 1 2 3 4 5		DK 1 2 3 4 5	
Market growth	DK 1 2 3 4 5		DK 1 2 3 4 5	
Competition	DK 1 2 3 4 5		DK 1 2 3 4 5	
Access to Port of Exit	DK 1 2 3 4 5		DK 1 2 3 4 5	
Access to international transportation network	DK 1 2 3 4 5		DK 1 2 3 4 5	

8. Were any of the BUSINESS CONDITIONS listed above IMPORTANT factors in your company's ORIGINAL DECISION TO SELL ITS PRODUCT ABROAD?

Yes___   No___   If YES, please list the two most important.

1._____   2._____

9. Please rate your opinion of the FAVORABILITY of the BUSINESS CONDITIONS for your company in the FIRST FOREIGN COUNTRY WHERE YOUR PRODUCTS WERE SOLD in year number one of product sales abroad and today. Please circle the number that applies. (DK= Don't know) Please indicate the country:_____

	Country Conditons in Year #1		Country Conditions Today	
	not favorable	favorable	not favorable	favorable
Economic conditions	DK 1 2 3 4 5		DK 1 2 3 4 5	
Tariffs and trade policies	DK 1 2 3 4 5		DK 1 2 3 4 5	
Language similarity	DK 1 2 3 4 5		DK 1 2 3 4 5	
Capital resources	DK 1 2 3 4 5		DK 1 2 3 4 5	
Experienced employees	DK 1 2 3 4 5		DK 1 2 3 4 5	
Raw materials and supplies	DK 1 2 3 4 5		DK 1 2 3 4 5	
Costs to enter market	DK 1 2 3 4 5		DK 1 2 3 4 5	
Size of market	DK 1 2 3 4 5		DK 1 2 3 4 5	
Growth of market	DK 1 2 3 4 5		DK 1 2 3 4 5	
Number of competitors	DK 1 2 3 4 5		DK 1 2 3 4 5	
Customer demand	DK 1 2 3 4 5		DK 1 2 3 4 5	
Transportation system	DK 1 2 3 4 5		DK 1 2 3 4 5	
Distribution network	DK 1 2 3 4 5		DK 1 2 3 4 5	
Geographic distance from U.S.	DK 1 2 3 4 5		DK 1 2 3 4 5	

10. Were any of the CONDITIONS listed above IMPORTANT factors IN YOUR COMPANY'S ORIGINAL DECISION to SELL ITS PRODUCTS ABROAD?
Yes ___ No ___ If YES, please list the two most important.

1._____ 2._____

11. Please rate the IMPORTANCE of the following REASONS why small businesses DECIDE TO SELL PRODUCTS ABROAD as they related to your company when this decision was first made. (DK= don't know)

	not important					important
To obtain new sources of capital	DK	1	2	3	4	5
To develop new markets	DK	1	2	3	4	5
To establish long term business relationships	DK	1	2	3	4	5
To be the first U.S. company in the market	DK	1	2	3	4	5
To overcome problems faced in domestic markets	DK	1	2	3	4	5
To reciprocate with suppliers abroad	DK	1	2	3	4	5
To fill customer orders for product	DK	1	2	3	4	5
To keep up with industry competitors	DK	1	2	3	4	5
To increase sales and profits	DK	1	2	3	4	5
To survive	DK	1	2	3	4	5
To obtain long term stability for the company	DK	1	2	3	4	5
To gain a large market share	DK	1	2	3	4	5
To capitalize on domestic competitive advantage	DK	1	2	3	4	5
Other (please specify)_____	DK	1	2	3	4	5

12. Please rate the IMPORTANCE of the following COMPANY CHARACTERISTICS as they related to your company when the decision TO SELL PRODUCTS ABROAD was first made. (DK= don't know)

The Company had:

	not important					important
well trained employees	DK	1	2	3	4	5
employees with international experience	DK	1	2	3	4	5
capital resources	DK	1	2	3	4	5
information about foreign markets	DK	1	2	3	4	5
cooperative arrangements with other small companies	DK	1	2	3	4	5
patented product technology	DK	1	2	3	4	5
innovative products	DK	1	2	3	4	5
quality products	DK	1	2	3	4	5
strong customer service capability	DK	1	2	3	4	5
low production costs	DK	1	2	3	4	5
economies of scale	DK	1	2	3	4	5
high growth in sales domestically	DK	1	2	3	4	5
high product acceptance domestically	DK	1	2	3	4	5
high profits from domestic sales	DK	1	2	3	4	5
planning systems in place	DK	1	2	3	4	5
the ability to adapt to market changes quickly	DK	1	2	3	4	5
standardized production operations	DK	1	2	3	4	5
flexible operations systems	DK	1	2	3	4	5
years of experience in domestic markets	DK	1	2	3	4	5
operated in slow growing industry domestically	DK	1	2	3	4	5

a large number of competitors domestically	DK	1 2 3 4 5
faced many new companies entering industry	DK	1 2 3 4 5
faced rapid technological changes domestically	DK	1 2 3 4 5
faced intense competition domestically	DK	1 2 3 4 5
operated in highly regulated domestic industry	DK	1 2 3 4 5
no competitive advantage in the U.S.	DK	1 2 3 4 5
other (please specify)_____	DK	1 2 3 4 5

13. Were YOU PERSONALLY INVOLVED in the company's DECISION TO SELL ITS PRODUCTS ABROAD?   Yes___ No ___   IF NO, please go to QUESTION # 21.

   a. If YES, please RATE THE IMPORTANCE of the following PERSONAL FACTORS
      as they related to your involvement in this decision.

	not important		important
You had:			
friends abroad	DK	1 2 3	4 5
relatives abroad	DK	1 2 3	4 5
business associates or contacts abroad	DK	1 2 3	4 5
customer contacts abroad	DK	1 2 3	4 5
government contacts abroad	DK	1 2 3	4 5
worked abroad	DK	1 2 3	4 5
studied abroad	DK	1 2 3	4 5
lived abroad	DK	1 2 3	4 5
travelled abroad	DK	1 2 3	4 5
marketing expertise	DK	1 2 3	4 5
technical knowledge	DK	1 2 3	4 5
financial management skills	DK	1 2 3	4 5
small business management expertise	DK	1 2 3	4 5
experience starting new businesses	DK	1 2 3	4 5
experience raising capital	DK	1 2 3	4 5
fluency in a foreign language	DK	1 2 3	4 5
a degree international business	DK	1 2 3	4 5
other (please specify)_____	DK	1 2 3	4 5

14. Please indicate the degree to which you DISAGREE or AGREE with the following
    statements: (DK = don't know)

	strongly disagree		strongly agree
Small businesses should be geographically unlimited from start-up	DK	1 2 3	4 5
Small businesses should sell their products abroad only after selling in U.S. markets	DK	1 2 3	4 5
Foreign markets offer unlimited opportunities for small businesses	DK	1 2 3	4 5
Selling products abroad is risky for small businesses	DK	1 2 3	4 5
Internationalization for a small business should be planned over time	DK	1 2 3	4 5
Small businesses should be quick to take advantage of international opportunities	DK	1 2 3	4 5

15. What are your company's PRESENT GOALS INTERNATIONALLY?

_____
_____
_____

4

16. If you EXPORT PRODUCTS, from which PORT(s) does your COMPANY SHIP most often? _____

17. Approximately what percentage of your company's INTERNATIONAL COMMUNICATIONS are sent by each of the following means: (The total should equal 100%)

Air Mail	____%	Computer	____%
Telephone	____%	FAX	____%
Overnight Express Mail	____%		
Other (please specify)	_____		

18. Which of the following best describe your company? (please check all that apply.)

sole proprietorship___   public corporation___   private corporation ___
"s" corporation ___   partnership ___   subsidiary ___
division or unit of another company ___   franchise ___
independently owned business ___   family-owned business ___

19. How many people did your company EMPLOY in past years?

	Year #1 of Sales Abroad	1989	1990
a. TOTAL number of employees	_____	_____	_____
b. FULL TIME (or equivalent) employees assigned in U.S.	_____	_____	_____
c. FULL TIME (or equivalent) employees assigned ABROAD	_____	_____	_____
d. PERCENTAGE employees assigned abroad who were U.S. citizens	_____	_____	_____

20. What were the approximate ANNUAL SALES, PERCENTAGE OF TOTAL SALES DERIVED FROM SALES OUTSIDE THE U.S., and RETURN ON SALES of your business for past years?

	Year #1 of Sales Abroad	1989	1990
a. TOTAL annual sales	$_____	$_____	$_____
b. PERCENTAGE of total sales derived from SALES OUTSIDE U.S.	_____%	_____%	_____%
c. RETURN ON TOTAL SALES	_____%	_____%	_____%

21. Were you involved in the FORMATION of this COMPANY? Yes___ No___

    a. If YES, what was your role? _____

    b. Is this your FIRST entrepreneurial effort?   Yes___   No ___
       If NO, how many other ventures have you tried? ____

5

c. Did you have PREVIOUS EXPERIENCE in the field of your business?
Yes___ No___ If YES, how many years? _____

d. What was your VISION of the SCOPE and FUTURE of the business at the time
the company was formed? _____
_____
_____
_____

e. What was the TOTAL INVESTMENT in your business at start-up?
personal $_____ other equity $_____ debt financing $_____

22. If you were NOT involved in the founding of this business, HOW DID YOU
BECOME INVOLVED in the MANAGEMENT of this company? (Please check one.)

purchased business___ hired by management___ succeeded family member___
inh rited business___ hired by owners ___ worked up through ranks___
other (please specify)_____

23. Were you previously EMPLOYED by a company where you worked OUTSIDE the
United States? Yes____ No ____ If YES, number of years ____

24. Do you have a CONTROLLING INTEREST in this company (greater than 50%)?
Yes____ No_____ Percent Owned_____

25. GENERAL CLASSIFICATION INFORMATION:

Your AGE: ____ Your GENDER: male ____ female _____

Highest LEVEL OF EDUCATION you have completed:_____
MAJOR FIELD of study _____

U.S. citizen: Yes___ No___ If no, in what country were you born?
_____

PREVIOUS OCCUPATION:_____ NUMBER OF YEARS:____

PRESENT TITLE:_____ NUMBER OF YEARS: ____

26. COMPANY CLASSIFICATION INFORMATION:

MAIN PRODUCT(S) sold by your company in the United States TODAY:_____
_____

MAIN INDUSTRY OF DOMESTIC OPERATIONS:_____

ZIP CODE where your MAIN OFFICE is LOCATED:_____

THANK YOU for your participation in this survey. Please check the appropriate box or
boxes and include your BUSINESS CARD if you would like:
[ ] to receive a copy of the summary results of this survey
[ ] to participate in a follow-up survey
[ ] to offer additional comments about small business internationalization
or discuss this survey by telephone.

6

Appendix F-1

Condition	Young	Old	Total
Economic conditions	3.0	2.6	2.7
Tax laws	2.2	2.0	2.0
Trade regulations	2.5	1.9	2.2
Foreign market information	2.3	2.0	2.1
Capital resources	2.3	2.3	2.3
Experienced employees	2.6	2.1	2.3
Raw materials and supplies	3.2	3.0	3.0
Customer demand	3.2	2.7	2.9
Market size	3.0	2.5	2.7
Market growth	3.1	4.0	2.7
Competition	2.9	2.7	2.8
Access to Port of Exit	3.4	2.9	3.1
Access to international transportation network	2.6	2.8	2.9

[1] mean values are based on respondents rating of domestic regional environment conditions in year one of internationalization. Scale 1 = unfavorable, 5 = very favorable. See Appendix E for copy of questionnaire.

Appendix F-1 (continued)

RANKING OF MOST IMPORTANT REGIONAL
ENVIRONMENT CONDITIONS q#10

Young
    1 Favorable customer demand
    2 Favorable market size
    3 Unfavorable customer demand

Old
    1 Favorable customer demand
    2 Favorable market growth
    3 Favorable market size

Total
    1 Favorable customer demand
    2 Favorable economic conditions
    3 Favorable market size
    4 Unfavorable economic conditions

Appendix F-2

PERCEIVED FAVORABILITY OF HOST COUNTRY
CONDITIONS IN YEAR ONE (q#9)[1]

Condition	Young	Old	Total
Economic conditions	2.8	2.4	2.5
Tariffs and trade policies	2.2	1.7	2.0
Language similarity	2.7	2.7	2.6
Capital resources	2.2	2.0	2.0
Experienced employees	2.3	2.0	2.1
Raw materials and supplies	2.1	2.3	2.2
Costs to enter market	2.6	2.5	2.5
Size of market	2.6	2.5	2.5
Growth of market	2.7	2.5	2.5
Number of competitors	2.7	2.6	2.6
Customer demand	3.1	2.8	2.9
Transportation system	2.6	2.6	2.5
Distribution network	2.2	2.4	2.2
Geographic distance from U.S.	2.6	2.5	2.5

[1] mean values are based on respondents rating of host country conditons year one of internationalization. Scale 1= unfavorable; 5 = very favorable. See Appendix E for copy of questionnaire.

Appendix F-2 (continued)

RANKING OF MOST IMPORTANT HOST
COUNTRY FACTORS (q#10)

Young   1 Favorable customer demand
                 2 Favorable economic conditions
                 3 Favorable size of market

Old   1 Favorable customer demand
                 2 Favorable market growth
                 3 Favorable economic conditions
                 4 Favorable language

Total   1 Favorable customer demand
                 2 Favorable market size
                 3 Favorable economic conditions

Appendix F-3

REASONS WHY SMALL BUSINESSES DECIDE TO SELL PRODUCTS ABROAD (q#11)[1]

Reason	Young	Old	Total
To obtain new sources of capital	2.72	1.8	2.07
To develop new markets	4.25	4.25	4.24
To establish long term business relationships	3.67	3.75	3.89
To be the first US company in the market	2.45	1.90	2.26
To overcome problems faced in domestic markets	2.59	2.30	2.40
To reciprocate with suppliers abroad	1.43	1.57	1.52
To fill customer orders for product	3.96	3.72	3.90
To keep up with industry competitors	2.79	2.51	2.72
To increase sales and profits	4.47	4.33	4.41
To survive	3.13	2.62	2.91
To obtain long term stability	3.61	3.30	3.49
To gain a large market share	3.62	3.46	3.23
To capitalize on domestic competitive advantage	3.24	1.88	3.14

[1] mean values are based on respondents rating of 1-5 for each item; 1= not important; 5= very important. See Appendix E for copy of questionnaire.

Appendix F-4

IMPORTANCE OF COMPANY AND INDUSTRY
FACTORS (q#12)[1]

Factor	Young	Old	Total
The Company had:			
well trained employees	2.6	2.8	2.8
employees with international experience	2.3	1.5	1.9
capital resources	2.4	2.5	2.4
information about foreign markets	2.8	2.5	2.7
cooperative arrangements			
with other small companies	1.7	1.5	1.6
patented product technology	2.3	1.8	2.1
innovative products	3.6	3.1	3.3
quality products	4.1	3.9	4.0
strong customer service capability	3.1	3.1	3.1
low production costs	2.8	2.5	2.7
economies of scale	2.3	2.3	2.3
high growth in sales domestically	2.5	2.4	2.5
high product acceptance domestically	3.1	3.2	3.2
high profits from domestic sales	2.4	2.5	2.5
planning systems in place	1.7	2.0	1.9
the ability to adapt to			
market changes quickly	3.1	2.7	2.9
standardized production operations	2.7	2.6	2.6
flexible operations systems	2.8	3.0	2.9
years of experience in domestic markets	2.7	3.2	2.9
operated in slow growing industry	2.5	2.7	2.5
many domestic competitors	2.4	2.6	2.4
many new companies entering industry	2.1	1.8	2.0
faced rapid technological changes	2.0	1.9	2.0
faced intense domestic competition	2.4	2.4	2.3
operated in highly regulated			
domestic industry	1.5	1.5	1.5
no competitive advantage in U.S.	1.8	1.6	1.7

[1] mean values are based on respondents rating of 1-5 for each item; 1=
   not important, 5 =very important. See Appendix E for questionnaire.

Appendix F-5

IMPORTANCE OF PERSONAL FACTORS (q#13)[1]

Factor	Young	Old	Total
You had:			
friends abroad	2.1	1.3	1.8
relatives abroad	1.3	1.0	1.2
business associates or contacts abroad	3.2	2.3	2.8
customer contacts abroad	3.6	3.0	3.2
government contacts abroad	1.5	1.5	1.5
worked abroad	1.4	1.3	1.3
studied abroad	1.2	1.2	1.2
lived abroad	1.3	1.2	1.3
travelled abroad	2.6	2.6	2.6
marketing expertise	3.1	2.8	2.9
technical knowledge	3.5	3.2	3.4
financial management skills	2.7	2.7	2.6
small business management expertise	3.1	3.3	3.2
experience starting new businesses	2.9	2.3	2.6
experience raising capital	2.3	1.9	2.1
fluency in a foreign language	1.6	1.8	1.7
a degree international business	1.0	1.4	1.2

1- mean values based on respondents ratings of 1-5 for each item; 1= not important; 5 = very important. See Appendix E for copy of questionnaire.

Bibliography

Aaby, N.E. & Slater, S.F.(1989)"Management Influences on Export Performance: A Review of Empirical Literature, *International Marketing Review,* 6:4, pp. 7-26

Abdel-Malek, T. (1978) "Export Marketing Orientation in Small Firms", *American Journal of Small Business*, 3:1, pp. 25-34

Adams, G. & Hall, G. (1993) "Influences on the Growth of SME's: An International Comparison", *Entrepreneurship and Regional Development,* 5:, pp. 73-84

Aharoni, Y. (1966) *The Foreign Investment Decision Process*, Boston: Harvard Business School

Aldrich, H., Woodward, W., & Rosen, B. (1987) "The Impact of Social Networks on Business Founding and Profit", in Churchill, N.C., Hornaday, J., Kirchoff, B., Krasner, O. & Vesper, K.H., (eds.) *Frontiers of Entrepreneurship Research*, Proceedings of the Babson College Conference on Entrepreneurship, Wellesley, MA, pp. 154-168

Aldrich, H.(1990) "Using and Ecological Perspective to Study Organization Founding Rates", *Entrepreneurship Theory and Practice*, 14:3, pp. 7-24

Ali, A. & Swiercz, P. (1991) "Firm Size and Export Behavior; Lessons From the Midwest", *Journal of Small Business Management*, 29:2, pp. 71-78

Akhter, S.H. & Friedman, R. (1989) "International Market Entry Strategies and Level of Involvement in Marketing Activities", in Negandhi, A.R. & Savara, A. (Eds.), *International Strategic Management*, Lexington, MA: D.C. Heath & Co., pp. 157-172

Anderson, O.H. (1993) "On the Internationalization Process of Firms: A Critical Analysis", *Journal of International Business Studies*, 24:2, pp. 209-231

Ayal, I. & Hirsch, S. (1982) "Marketing Factors in Small Country Manufactured Exports: Are Market Share and Market Growth Rate Really Important?", *Journal of International Business Studies*, 16:2, pp. 73-85

Bain, J.S. (1968) *Industrial Organization*, New York: John Wiley

Baird, I., Lyles, M.A., & Orris, J.B. (1994) "The Choice of International Strategies by Small Businesses", *Journal of Small Business Management*, 32:1, pp. 48-59

Barrett, N.J. & Wilkinson, I. (1985) "Export Stimulation : A Segmentation Study of the Exporting Problems of Australian Manufacturing Firms", *European Journal of Marketing, 19:2, pp. 53-71*

Beamish, P.W. & Munro, H. (1986) "The Export Performance of Small and Medium-sized Canadian Manufacturers", *Canadian Journal of Administrative Science*, 3:1, pp. 29-40

Berger, P.L. & Luckman, T. (1967) *The Social Construction of Reality*, New York: Anchor Press (Doubleday)

Bilkey, W.J. (1978) "An Attempted Integration of the Literature on the Export Behavior of Firms", *Journal of International Business Studies*, 9:1, pp. 33-46

Bilkey, W.J. & Tesar, G. (1977) "The Export Behavior of Smaller-Sized Wisconsin Manufacturing Firms", *Journal of International Business Studies*, 8:1, pp. 93-98

Bijmolt, T.H. & Zwart, P.S. (1994) "The Impact of Internal Factors on the Export Success of Dutch Small-Medium Sized Firms" *Journal of Small Business Management*, 32:2, pp. 69-83

Birch,D. (1987), *Job Creation in America,* New York: Free Press

Bird, B. (1989), *Entrepreneurial Behavior*, Glenview, Ill: Scott Foresman

Bird, B. (1992) "The Operation of Intentions in Time: The Emergence of the New Venture", *Entrepreneurship Theory and Practice*, 17:1, pp. 11-20

Bradley, M.F. (1987) "Nature and Significance of International Marketing", *Journal of Business Research*, 15: pp. 205-219

Brockhaus, R.H. (1980) "Risk-Taking Propensity of Entrepreneurs", *Academy of Management Journal*, 23: pp. 509-520

Brush, C.G. & VanderWerf, P. (1992) "A Comparison of Methods and Sources for Obtaining Estimates of New Venture Performance", *Journal of Business Venturing*, 7:2, pp. 157-170

Brush, C.G. & Peters, M.P. (1992) "The Impact of Market Information Scanning Practices on the Performance of New Service and Manufacturing Ventures", Unpublished Working Paper, Boston College

Buckley, P.J. & Casson, J. (1978) "A Theory of International Operations", in Ghertman, M. & Leontiades, J. (eds.), *European Research in International Business*, Amsterdam: North Holland Publishing Co., pp. 1-8

Buckley, P.J. (1983) "New Theories of International Business: Some Unresolved Issues", in Casson, M. (ed.), *The Growth of International Business*, London: George Allen & Unwin, pp. 34-50

Buckley, P.J. (1988) "The Limits of Explanation: Testing the Internalization Theory of the Multinational Enterprise", *Journal of International Business Studies*, 19:1, pp. 181-193

Buckley, P.J. (1989) "Foreign Market Servicing Strategies and Competitiveness: A Theoretical Framework", in Negandhi, A.R. & Savara, A. (eds.), *International Strategic Management*, Lexington, MA: D.C. Heath & Co., pp. 69-88

Buckley, P.J. & Brooke, M.Z. (1992) *International Business Studies: An Overview*, Cambridge, MA: Blackwell Publishing

Bull, I. & Willard, G. (1993) "Towards a Theory of Entrepreneurship", *Journal of Business Venturing*, 8:3, pp. 183-196

Bygrave, W.D. (1989) "The Entrepreneurship Paradigm (11): Chaos and Catastrophes Among Quantum Jumps?" *Entrepreneurship Theory and Practice*, 14:2, pp. 7-30

Bygrave, W.D. & Hofer, C.W. (1991) "Theorizing About Entrepreneurship", *Entrepreneurship Theory and Practice*, 16:2, pp. 13-22

Calof, J.L. (1993) "The Impact of Size on Internationalization",*Journal of Small Business Management, 31:4, pp. 66-69*

Carmines, E.G. & Zeller, R.A. (1985) *Reliability and Validity Assessment*, Beverly Hills, CA: Sage University Press

Casson, M. (1979) *Alternatives to the Multinational Enterprise*, London: MacMillan Press Ltd.

Casson, M. (ed.) (1983a) *The Growth of International Business*, London: George Allen & Unwin

Casson, M. (1983b) "Introduction: The Conceptual Framework", in Casson, M. (ed.) *The Growth of International Business*, London: George Allen & Unwin, pp. 1-33

Cateora, P.R. & Hess, J.M. (1975) *International Marketing*, 3rd Edition, Homewood Ill., Richard D. Irwin

Caves, R.E. (1982) *Multinational Enterprise and Economic Analysis*, New York: Cambridge University Press

Cavusgil, S.T. & Nevin, J.R. (1981) "Internal Determinants of Export Marketing Behavior", *Journal of Marketing Research*, 18:2, pp. 114-119

Cavusgil, S.T. (1982) "Some Observations on the Relevance of Critical Variables for Internationalization Stages", in Czinkota, M.R. & Tesar, G. (eds.) *Export Management: An International Context*, New York: Praeger, pp. 276-287

Cavusgil, S.T. (1984a) "Organizational Characteristics Associated with Export Activity", *Journal of Management Studies*, 21:1, pp. 3-22

Cavusgil, S.T. (1984b) "Differences Among Exporting Firms Based on Their Degree of Internationalization", *Journal of Business Research*, 12:2, pp. 195-208

Cavusgil, S.T. & Nevin, J.R. (1981) "Internal Determinants of Export Marketing Behavior: An Empirical Investigation", *Journal of Marketing Research*, 18:1, pp. 114-119

Cavusgil, S.T. & Naor, J.(1987) "Firm Management Characteristics as Discriminators of Export Marketing Activity", *Journal of Business Research*, 15:3, pp. 221-235

Chandler, A.D., Jr.(1962) *Strategy and Structure: Chapters in the History of American Industrial Enterprise*, Cambridge, MA: MIT Press

Chatterjee, S. (1990) "Excess Resources, Utilization Costs and Mode of Entry", *Academy of Management Journal*, 33:4, pp. 780-800

Christensen, C.H., da Rocha, A. & Gertner, R.K. (1987) "An Empirical Investigation of the Factors Influencing Export Success of Brazilian Firms", *Journal of International Business Studies*, Fall, pp. 61-77

Christensen, P.R. (1991) "The Small and Medium-sized Exporters Squeeze: Empirical Evidence and Model Reflections", *Entrepreneurship and Regional Development*, 3:, pp. 49-65

Churchill, G.A. Jr. (1979) "A Paradigm for Developing Better Measures of Marketing Constructs", *Journal of Marketing Research,* 16: pp. 64-73

Churchill, N.C. & Lewis, V.(1983) "The Five Stages of Small Business Growth", *Harvard Business Review*, 61:3, pp. 30-50

Clegg, J. (1990) "The Determinants of Aggregate International Liscensing Behavior-Evidence from Five Countries", *Management International Review*, 30:3, pp. 231-251

Cole, A.H. (1965) "An Approach to the Study of Entrepreneurship: A Tribute to Edwin F. Gay", in Aitken, H.G. (ed.), *Explorations in Enterprise*, Cambridge, MA: Harvard University Press, pp. 30-44

Contractor, F.J. (1990) "Contractual and Cooperative Forms of International Business: Towards a Unified Theory of Modal Choice", *Management International Review*, 30:1, pp. 31-54

Contractor, F.J. (1989) "Ownership Patterns of U.S. Joint Ventures Abroad and the Liberalization of Foreign Government Regulations in the 1980's: Evidence from the Benchmark Surveys", *Journal of International Business Studies*, 21:1, pp. 55-73

Cooper, A.C. (1981), "Strategic Management: New Ventures and Small Businesses", *Long Range Planning*, 14:5, pp. 39-45

Cooper, A.C. & Dunkelberg, W.C. (1986) "Entrepreneurship and Paths to Business Ownership", *Strategic Management Journal*, 7: pp. 53-68

Cooper, A.C., Woo, C. & Dunkelberg, W.C. (1989) "Entrepreneurship and the Initial Size of Firms", *Journal of Business Venturing*, 4:5, pp. 317-332

Cooper, R.G. & Kleinschmidt, E.J. (1985) "The Impact of Export Strategy on Export Sales Performance", *Journal of International Business Studies*, 16:1, pp. 37-55

Cyert, R.M. & March, J.G. (1963) *A Behavioral Theory of the Firm* Englewood Cliffs, NJ: Prentice Hall

Czinkota, M.R. & Johnston, W.J. (1981) "Segmenting U.S. Firms for Export Development", *Journal of Business Research*, 9:4, pp. 353-365

Czinkota, M.R. & Tesar, G. (eds.) (1982) *Export Management: An International Context*, New York: Praeger Publishing

Czinkota, M.R. & Johnston, W.J. (1983) "Exporting: Does Sales Volume Make a Difference?" *Journal of International Business Studies*, 14:1, pp. 147-153

Daniels, J.D. (1983) "Combining Strategic and International Business", *Management International Review*, 23:3, p. 4-15

Daniels, J.D., Pitts, R. & Tretter, M.J. (1985) "Organizing for Dual Strategies of Product Diversity and International Expansion", *Strategic Management Journal*, 6: pp. 223-237

Dean, T. & Meyer, D. (1989) "Venture Development in High-Technology Firms: The Impact of Managerial Quoties Across the Organizational Life Cycle" in Brockhaus, R.H. Sr.; Churchill, N.C. Katz, J.A.; Kirchoff, B.A., Vesper, K.N., & Wetzel, W.E. Jr., (eds.) *Frontiers of Entrepreneurship Research*, Proceedings of the Babson College Conference, Wellesley, MA: Babson College. pp.93-108

Denis, J.E. & Depelteau, D. (1985) "Market Knowledge Diversification and Export Expansion", *Journal of International Business Studies*, 16:3, pp. 77-89

Denzin, N.K. (1978) *The Research Act: A Theoretical Introduction to Sociological Methods*, 2nd Ed., New York: McGraw Hill

Dollinger, M. (1985) "Environmental Contacts and Performance of the Smaller Firm", *Journal of Small Business Management*, 23:1, pp. 24-30

Dominguez, L.& Sequeira, C.. (1993) "Determinants of LDC Exporters Performance: A Cross National Study" *Journal of International Business Studies*, 24:1, pp. 19-40

Donckels, R. (1989) "New Entrepreneurship: Lessons from the Past, Perspectives for the Future", *Entrepreneurship and Regional Development*, 1:1, pp. 75-84

Drucker, P.F. (1985) *Innovation and Entrepreneurship*, New York: Harper & Row

D'Souza, D. & McDougall, P.P. (1989) "Third World Joint Venturing: A Strategic Option for the Smaller Firm", *Entrepreneurship Theory and Practice*, Summer, pp. 19-33

D'Souza, D. & Eramilli, M. (1991) "Market Entry Behavior of Small Firms: Some Empirical Evidence", paper presented at the Babson College Conference on Entrepreneurship Research, Pittsburgh, PA

D'Souza, D. & Eramilli, M. (1993) "Venturing into Foreign Markets: The Case of the Small Service Firm", *Entrepreneurship Theory and Practice*, 17:4, pp. 29-41

Dunning, J.H. (1974) (Ed.) *Economic Analysis and the Multinational Enterprise*, London, George Allen & Unwin

Dunning, J.H. (1979) "The Distinctive Nature of the Multinational Enterprise", in Dunning, J.H. (ed.) *Economic Analysis and the Multinational Enterprise*, New York: Praeger Publishing, pp. 1-12

Dunning, J. (1988) "The Eclectic Paradigm of International Production: A Restatement and Some Possible Extensions", *Journal of International Business Studies*, Spring, pp. 1-31

Eglehoff, W.G. (1988) "Strategy and Structure in Multinational Corporations: A Revision of Stopford and Wells Model", *Strategic Management Journal*, 9: pp. 1-14

Eggers, J., Leahy, K. & Churchill, N.C. (1994) "Stages of Small Business Growth Revisited: Insights into Growth Path and Leadership Management Skills in Low and High Growth Companies", presented at Babson Entrepreneurship Research Conference, Babson College, Wellesley, MA

Eisenhardt, K. (1992), "Speed and Strategic Choice: How Managers Accelerate Decision-making", *California Management Review*, 32:3, pp. 39-54

Eramilli, M.K. & Rao, C.P. (1994) "Choice of Foreign Market Entry Mode by Service Firms: The Role of Market Knowledge" *Management International Review*, 30:2, pp. 135-150

Erdos, P.L. (1970) *Professional Mail Surveys*, New York: McGraw Hill

Faucett, J. (1988) "Small Business Exports of Manufactured Products, 1985", Final Report to the Office of Advocacy, U.S. Small Business Administration, Washington, D.C., SBA Contract 2066-AER 87

Fayerweather, J. (1978) *International Business Strategy and Administration*, Cambridge, MA: Ballinger

Feeser, H.R. & Willard, G.E. (1990), "Founding Strategy and Performance: A Comparison of High and Low Growth High Tech Firms", *Strategic Management Journal*, 11, pp. 87-98

Ford, D. & Rosson, P. (1982) "The Relationships Between Export Manufacturers and Their Overseas Distributors", in Czinkota, M.R. & Tesar, G., (eds.) *Export Management: An International Context*, pp. 257-275

Fowler, F.J. (1988) *Survey Research Methods*, Revised Ed., Beverly Hills, CA: Sage Publications

Frank, H., Plaschka, G., & Roessl, D. (1989) "Planning Behavior of Successful and Non-Successful Founders of New Ventures", *Entrepreneurship and Regional Development*, 1:1 pp. 191-200

Fredriksen, C., Klofsten, M., Olofsson, C. & Wahlbin, C. (1989) "Growth, Performance and Financial Structure of New Technology-Based Firms", in Brockhaus, R. Sr., Churchill, N.C., Katz, J.A., Kirchoff, B.A., Vesper, R.A., & Wetzel, W.E. Jr. (eds.) *Frontiers of Entrepreneurship Research*, Proceedings of the Babson Conference, Wellesley, MA: Babson College, pp. 189-199

Galbraith, C. & Stiles, C. (1983) "Firm Profitability and Relative Firm Power", *Strategic Management Journal*, 4, pp. 237-249

Galbraith, C.S., DeNoble, A.F. & Estavillo, P. (1990) "Location Criteria and Perceptions of Regional Business Climate: A Study of Mexican and U.S. Small Electronics Firms", *Journal of Small Business Management*, 28:4, pp. 34-47

Gartner, W.B. (1985) "A Conceptual Framework for Describing the Phenomenon of New Venture Creation", *Academy of Management Review*, 14:4, pp. 696-706

Gartner, W.B., Bird, B.J. & Starr, J.A. (1992) "Acting As If: Differentiating Entrepreneurial Behavior from Organizational Behavior", *Entrepreneurship Theory and Practice*, 16:3, pp 13-33

Geringer, J.M., Beamish, P.W. & daCosta, R.C. (1989) "Diversification Strategy and Internationalization: Implications for MNE Performance", *Strategic Management Journal,* 10, pp. 109-119

Giamartino, G., McDougall, P. & Bird, B. (1993) "International Entrepreneurship: The State of the Field", *Entrepreneurship Theory & Practice*, Fall, pp. 37-42

Gibb, A. & Scott, M. (1985) "Strategic Awareness, Personal Commitment, and the Process of Planning in Small Business", *Journal of Management Studies, 22: pp. 597-631*

Ginn, C.W. & Sexton, D.L. (1990) " A Comparison of the Personality Type Dimension of 1987 *Inc.* 500 Company Founder/CEO's with those of Slower-Growth Firms", *Journal of Business Venturing*, 5:5, pp. 313-326

Gomes-Casseres, B. & Kohn, T. (1990) "Global Competition by Small Technology-Based Firms", Working Paper, Harvard Business School; 89-070

Goodnow, J.D. & Hansz, J.E. (1972) "Environmental Determinants of Overseas Market Entry Strategies", *Journal of International Business Studies*, 3:1, pp. 33-50

Goslin, L.N. (1987), "Characteristics of Successful High-Tech Start-up Firms" in Churchill, N.C., Hornaday, J.A., Kirchoff, B.A., Krasner, O.J., & Vesper, K.H. (eds.) *Frontiers of Entrepreneurship Research*, Proceedings of the Babson College Conference on Entrepreneurship, Wellesley, MA: Babson College, pp. 452-463

Green, R.T. & Cunningham, W.H. (1975) "The Determinants of U.S. Foreign Investment: An Empirical Examination", *Management International Review*, 15: 2-3, pp. 113-120

Greiner, L.E. (1972) "Evolution and Revolution as Organizations Grow", *Harvard Business Review,* 50:4, pp. 37-46

Gripsrud, G. (1989) "The Determinants of Export Decisions and Attitudes to a Distant Market: Norwegian Fishery Exports to Japan", *Journal of International Business Studies*, 21:3, pp. 469-485

Hair, J.F., Jr., Anderson, R.E. & Tatham, R.L., *Multivariate Data Analysis*, 2nd Edition, New York: MacMillan Publishing

Hambrick, D. & Mason, P.A. (1984) "Upper Echelons: The Organization as a Reflection of its Top Manager's" *Academy of Management Review,* 9:2, pp 193-206

Harrigan, K. (1983) "Research Methodologies for Contingency Approaches to Business Strategy", *Academy of Management Review*, 8:3, pp. 398-405

Harrigan, K. (1985) "Vertical Integration and Corporate Strategy", *Academy of Management Journal,* 28:2, pp. 397-425

Hill, C.W.L., Hwang, P. & Kim, W.C. (1990) "An Eclectic Theory of the Choice of Entry Mode", *Strategic Management Journal*, 11, pp. 117-128

Hinrichs, J.R. (1975) "Effects of Sampling Follow-up Letters and Commitment to Participate on a Mail Attitude Survey Response", *Journal of Applied Psychology,* 60:2, pp 249-257.

Hirsch, S. & Adar, Z. (1974) "Firm Size and Export Performance" *World Development*, 2:7, pp. 41-46

Hisrich, R.D. & Peters, M.P. (1983) "East-West Trade: An Assessment by U.S. Manufacturers", *Columbia Journal of World Business*, 18: 4, pp. 44-50

Holziger, A.G. (1990a) "Reach New Markets", *Nation's Business*, Dec. pp. 18-27

Holziger, A.G. (1990b) "More Progress in East-West Trade", *Nation's Business*, June, pp. 33-38

Holziger, A.G. (1990c) "Eastern Europe: A New Frontier", *Nation's Business*, April, pp. 45-49

Holzmuller, H. & Kasper, H. (1991) "Ona a Theory fo Export Performance: Personal and Organizational Determinants of Export Trade Activities Observed in Small and Medium-Sized Firms", *Management International Review*, Special Issue, pp. 45-70

Horst, T. (1979),"The Theory of the Firm", in Dunning, J.H. (ed.) *Economic Analysis and the Multinational Enterprise*, New York: Praeger Publishing, pp. 31-46

Hoslitz, B.F. (1962) "Entrepreneurship and Economic Growth", *American Journal of Economic Sociology* 3:4, pp. 93-100

Huber, G.G. (1985) "Temporal Stability and Response Order Bias in Participant Descriptions of Organizational Decisions", *Academy of Management Journal*, 28:4, pp. 943-950

Hustedde, P.J. & Pulver, G.C. (1992) "Factors Affecting Equity Capital Acquisition: The Demand Side", *Journal of Business Venturing*, 7:5, pp. 363-374]

Hymer, S. (1960) "The International Operations of National Firms: A Study of Direct Investment", Unpublished Doctoral Dissertation, MIT

Ireland, R.D. & Van Auken, P. (1987) "Entrepreneurship and Small Business Research: An Historical Topology and Directions for Future Research", *American Journal of Small Business*, 11:4, pp. 9-20

Johanson J. & Vahlne, J.E. (1977) "The Internationalization Process of the Firm--A Model of Knowledge Development and Increasing Foreign Market Commitment", *Journal of International Business Studies*, 8:1, pp. 23-32

Johnston, W.J. & Czinkota, M.R. (1982) "Managerial Motivations as Determinants of Industrial Export Behavior", in Czinkota, M.R. & Tesar, G., (eds.) *Export Management: An International Context*, New York: Praeger Press

Kao, J. (1989) *Entrepreneurship, Creativity and Organization*, Englewood Cliffs, NJ: Prentice Hall

Katz, J. & Gartner, W. B. (1988) "Properties of Emerging Organizations", *Academy of Management Review*, 13:3, pp. 429-441

Katz, J. (1992) "A Psycho-Social Cognitive Model of Employment Status Choice", *Entrepreneurship Theory and Practice*, 17:1, pp. 29-38

Kaynak, E. (1992) "A Cross Regional Comparison of Export Performance of Two Firms in Two Canadian Regions", *Management International Review*, 33:1, pp. 43-63

Kazanjian, R.K. & Drazin, R. (1990) "A Stage Contingent Model of Size and Growth for Technologically Based Ventures", *Journal of Business Venturing*, 5:3, pp. 137-150

Kedia, B. & Chokar, J. (1986) "Factors Inhibiting Export Performance of Firms: An Empirical Investigation", *Management International Review*, 26:4, pp. 33-43

Keeley, R.H. & Roure, J.B., Goto, M., Yoshimura, K. (1990) "An International Comparison of New Ventures"; in Churchill, N.C., Bygrave, W.D., Hornaday, J.A., Muzyka, D.F., Vesper, K.H., & Wetzel, W.E. (eds.) *Frontiers of Entrepreneurship Research*, Proceedings of the Babson College Conference on Entrepreneurship; Wellesley, MA; Babson College, pp. 472-480

Kent, C.A., Sexton, D.L. & Vesper, K.H.(eds.) (1982) *Encyclopedia of Entrepreneurship*, Englewood Cliffs, NJ: Prentice Hall

Kent, C.A. (1982) "Entrepreneurship and Economic Development" in Kent, C.A., Sexton, D.L. & Vesper, K.H.(eds.) (1982) *Encyclopedia of Entrepreneurship*, Englewood Cliffs, NJ: Prentice Hall, pp. 237-253

Kerlinger, F.N. (1964) *Foundations of Behavioral Research,* 2nd ed., New York: Holt, Rinehart & Winston, Inc.

Kidder, L.H. & Judd C.M. (1986) *Research Methods in Social Relations*, 5th ed., New York: Holt Rinehart & Winston

Kindleberger, C.P. (1969) *American Business Abroad: Six Lectures on Direct Investment*, New Haven, CT: Yale University Press

Kirchoff, B. & Phillips, B. (1987) "Examining Entrepreneurship's Role in Economic Growth", in Churchill, N.C., Hornaday, J.A., Kirchoff, B., Krasner, O.J. & Vesper, K. (eds.) *Frontiers of Entrepreneurship Research*, Wellesley, MA Babson College, pp. 57-71

Kirchoff, B. & Phillips, B. (1988),"The Effect of Firm Formation and Growth on Job Creation in the United States", *Journal of Business Venturing*, 3:4, pp. 261-272

Kirchoff, B.A. (1991) "Entrepreneurship's Contribution to Economics", *Entrepreneurship Practice and Theory*, 16:2, pp. 93-112

Kirplani, V.H. & MacIntosh, N.B. (1980) "Internal Marketing Effectiveness of Technology-Oriented Small Firms", *Journal of International Business Studies*, 11: (Winter) pp. 81-90.

Kirzner, I. (1982) "The Theory of Entrepreneurship in Economic Growth" in Kent, C.A., Sexton, D.L. & Vesper, K.H.(eds.) (1982) *Encyclopedia of Entrepreneurship*, Englewood Cliffs, NJ: Prentice Hall, pp. 272-277

Klecka, W.R. (1980) *Discriminant Analysis*, Beverly Hills, CA: Sage Publications

Knickerbocker, F. T. (1973) *Oligopolostic Reaction and the MNE,* Cambridge, MA: Harvard Press

Knight, F. (1921) *Risk, Uncertainty, and Profit* (1964 reprint) New York, A.M. Kelly

Kobrin, S.J. (1987) "Testing the Bargaining Hypothesis in the Manufacturing Sector in Developing Countries", *International Organization*, 41:4, pp. 609-638

Kogut, B. (1985), "Designing Global Strategies: Profiting from Operational Flexibility", *Sloan Management Review,* Fall, pp. 27-38

Kogut, B. & Singh, H. (1988), "The Effect of National Culture on the Choice of Entry Mode", *Journal of International Business Studies*, Fall, pp. 411-432

Kohn, T. (1988) *International Entrepreneurship: Foreign Direct Investment by Small U.S.-Based Manufacturing Firms*, Doctoral Dissertation, Harvard University Graduate School of Management

Kothari, V. (1978) "Strategic Approaches of Small U.S. Manufacturers in International Markets", in Susbauer, J. (ed.), *Academy of Management Proceedings*, 38th Meeting, pp. 362-366

Lahti, A. (1989) "A Contingency Theory of Entrepreneurial Strategy for a Small Scale Company Operating from a Small and Open Economy in Open European Competition", *Entrepreneurship and Regional Development*, 1:3, pp. 221-236

Larson, A. (1992) "NEtwork Dyads in Entrepreneurial Settings: A Study of the Governance of Exchange Relationships", *Administrative Sciences Quarterly*, 37: pp. 76-104

Lecraw, D.J. (1984) "Diversification Strategy and Performance", *The Journal of Industrial Economics*, 33:2, pp. 179-198

Lecraw, D.J. (1989) "The Management of Countertrade: Factors Influencing Success", *Journal of International Business Studies*, 20:1, pp. 41-59

Liebenstein, H. (1968) "Entrepreneurship and Development" *American Economic Review*, 58:2, pp. 72-83

Lim, J.S., Sharkey, T.W. & Kim, K.I. (1991) "An Empirical Test of an Export Adoption Model", *Management International Review*, pp. 51-62

Liouville, J. (1992) "Under What Conditions Can Exports Exert a Positive Influence on Profitability", *Management International Review*, 32:1, pp. 41-54

Lindquist, M.C. (1990) "Critical Success Factors in the Process of Internationalization of Small Hi-Tech Firms", in Birley, S. (ed.) *Building European Ventures*, published by European Foundation for Entrepreneurship Research, Elsevier, pp. 36-60

Lippitt, G. & Schmidt, W. (1967) "Crises in a Developing Organization" *Harvard Business Review*, Nov.- Dec., pp. 102-112

Lorange, P. & Roos, J. (1990) "Formation of Cooperative Ventures: Competence Mix of Management Teams", *Management International Review*, Special Issue, pp. 69-86

Macharzina, K. & Englehard, J. (1991) "Paradigm Shift in International Business: Research from Partist and Eclectic Approaches to the Gains Paradigm", *Management International Review*, Special Issue, pp. 23-43

Malekzadeh, A.R., & Nahavandi, A. (1984) "Small Business Exporting: Misconceptions are Abundant", *American Journal of Small Business*, 9:4, pp. 7-14

Marchesnay, M. & Julien, P. A. (1990) "The Small Business: as a Transaction Space", *Entrepreneurship and Regional Development*, 2:3 pp. 267-277

Mascarenhas, B. (1986) "International Strategies of Non-Dominant Firms", *Journal of International Business Studies*, Spring, pp. 1-25

Maynard, R. (1994) "A Good Time to Export", *Nation's Business*, May, pp. 22-32

McClelland, D. (1961) *The Achieving Society*, New York: The Free Press

McDougall, P.P. (1989) "International Versus Domestic Entrepreneurship: New Venture Strategic Behavior and Industry Structure", *Journal of Business Venturing*, 4, pp. 387-399

McDougall, P.P., Oviatt, B. & Brush, C. (1991) "A Symposium on Global Start-ups: Entrepreneurial Firms that are Born International", presentation at the Entrepreneurship Division of the National Academy of Management Meetings

McDougall, P.P., Shane, S. & Oviatt, B.M. (forthcoming) "Explaining the Formation of International New Ventures: The Limits of Theories from International Business Research", *Journal of Business Venturing*

McGuire, J.W. (1976) "The Small Enterprise in Economics and Organizational Theory", *Journal of Contemporary Business*, 15:3, pp. 165-188

McMullan, W.E. & Long, W.A. (1990) *Developing New Ventures: The Entrepreneurial Option*, Orlando, FL Harcourt Brace Jovanovich

Melin, L. (1992) "Internationalization as a Strategy Process", *Strategic Management Journal*, 13: Winter, Special Issue, pp. 99-118

Merton, R.K. (1962) *Social Theory and Social Structure*, New York: The Free Press

Miesenbock, K.J. (1988) "Small Businesses and Exporting: A Literature Review", *International Small Business Journal*, Jan-Mar., pp. 42-63

Miller, D. (1983) "The Correlates of Entrepreneurship in Three Types of Firms", *Management Science*, 29:7, pp. 770-791

Mintzberg, H. (1978) "Patterns in Strategy Formulation", *Management Science*, 29:4, pp. 934-948

Mitton, Daryl, (1989) "The Complete Entrepreneur", *Entrepreneurship Theory and Practice*, 13:3, pp. 9-19

Morrison, A.J. & Roth, K. (1989) "International Business-Level Strategy: The Development of a Holistic Model", in Negandhi, A.R. & Savara, A. (eds.) *International Strategic Management*, Lexington, MA: D.C. Heath & Co., pp. 29-52

Morrison, D. (1969) "Discriminant Analysis", *Journal of Marketing Research*, VI, May, pp. 156-163

Namiki, N. (1988) "Export Strategy for Small Business", *Journal of Small Business Management*, 26:2, pp. 33-37

Norusis, M. J. (1987) *The SPSS Guide to Data Analysis for SPSSX*, Chicago, ILL: SPSS, Inc.

Nunnally, J.C. (1970) *Introduction to Psychological Measurement*, New York: McGraw Hill

Olson, C.H., & Weidersheim-Paul, F. (1978) "Factors Affecting the Pre-export Behavior of Non-exporting Firms", (eds.) in Ghertman, M. & Leontiades, J. *European Research in International Business,* pp. 283-305

O'Rourke, A.D. (1985) "Differences in Exporting Practices, Attitudes and Problems by Size of Firm", *American Journal of Small Business*, 9:3, pp. 25-29

Oviatt, B.M. & McDougall, P.P. (1994) "Toward a Theory of International New Ventures", *Journal of International Business Studies*, 25:1, pp. 45-63

Oviatt, B.M., McDougall, P.P. & Dinterman, T. (1993) "Global Start-ups: Forces Driving Their Growth and Patterns of Success", Presented at Babson Conference on Entrepreneurship Research, May, 1993

Pak, J. & Weaver, K.M. (1990) "Differences Among Small Manufacturing Firms Based on their Level of Export Involvement: Potential, Opportunistic and Strategic Exporters", *Proceedings of the USASBE Conference*, (eds.) Garsombke, T.W. & Garsombke, D.J., pp. 119-125

Palmer, M. (1971) "The Application of Psychological Testing to Entrepreneurial Potential", *California Management Review,* 13:3, pp 32-38

Parsons, T. & Smelser, N. J. (1956) *Economy and Society*, Glencoe, ILL: The Free Press

Payne, J. (1973) *Principles of Social Science Measurement*, College Station, Texas: Lytton Publishing

Penner, K. (1990) "Industrial Policy", *Business Week*, April 6, p.70

Perlmutter, H.V. (1969) "The Tortuous Evolution of the Multinational Corporation", *Columbia Journal of World Business*, pp. 9-18

Pezeshkpur, C. (1979) "A Systematic Approach to Finding Export Opportunities", *Harvard Business Review*, Sept.- Oct., pp. 182-196

Piercy, N. (1981) "Company Internationalization: Active and Reactive Exporting", *European Journal of Marketing*, 15:3, pp. 26-40

Porter, M. (ed.) (1986) *Competitive Advantage in Global Industries*, Boston: Harvard Business School Press

Rabino, S. (1980) "An Examination of Barriers to Exporting Encountered by Small Manufacturing Companies", *Management International Review*, 20:1, pp. 67-73

Ray, D. (1991) " Reconfiguring Small Business Exports: Shifting the Paradigm Towards New Venture Development and Internationalization", Unpublished Working Paper

Reid, S.D. (1980) "A Behavioral Approach to Export Decision Making", in Bagozzi, R., Bernhardt, K., Busch, P., Cravens, D., Hair, J. & Scott, C. (eds.) *Marketing in the 80's*, Educators Conference Series, pp. 265-268

Reid, S.D. (1981) "The Decision-maker and Export Entry and Expansion", *Journal of International Business Studies*, 12:2. pp.101-112

Reid, S.D. (1984) "Information Acquisition and Export Entry Decisions in Small Firms", *Journal of Business Research,* 12:2, pp. 141-157

Reynolds, P.D. (1991) "Sociology and Entrepreneurship: Concepts and Contributions", *Entrepreneurship Theory and Practice*, 16:2, pp. 47-70

Rice, G.H. & Hamilton, R.E. (1979) Decision Theory and the Small Business, *American Journal of Small Business,* 4: pp. 1-7

Robinson, R. & Pearce, J.A. (1984) "Research Thrusts in Small Firm Strategic Planning", *Academy of Management Review,* 9:1, pp. 1-4

Robock, S. & Simmonds, K. (1983) *International Business and Multinational Enterprises*, Homewood, Ill: Richard D. Irwin

Romanelli, E. (1989) "Environments and Strategies of Organizations at Start-up: Effects on Early Survival", *Administrative Sciences Quarterly*, 34: pp. 269-387

Root, F. (1993) "A Retrospective Look at International Business as a Field of Study", remarks from paper entitled "Some Reflections on the Evolution of International Business as a Field of Study: From Periphery to Center", in Nigh, D. & Toyne, B. (eds.) *International Busioness: Institutions and Dissemination of Knowledge,* Columbia S.C.: University of South Carolina Press, forthcoming

Roy, D.A. & Simpson, C.L. (1981) "Export Attitudes of Business Executives in the Smaller Manufacturing Firm", *Journal of Small Business Management*, 19:2, pp. 16-22

Rugman, A. (1971) "Risk Reduction by International Diversification", *Journal of International Business Strategy*, 7, pp. 75-80

Rugman, A. (1979) *International Diversification and the Multinational Enterprise*, Lexington, MA: Lexington Books

Samuels, J., Greenfield, S. & Mpuku, H. (1992) "Exporting and the Smaller Firm", *International Small Business Journal*, pp. 24-36

Sandberg, W. (1984) *New Venture Performance: The Role of Strategy and Industry Structure*, Lexington, MA: Lexington Books

Sandberg, W. (1992) "Strategic Management's Potential Contributions to a Theory of Entrepreneurship", *Entrepreneurship Theory and Practice*, 16:3, pp. 73-90

Schumpeter, J. (1942) *Capitalism, Socialism and Democracy,* New York: Harper and Row

Scott, M. & Bruce, R. (1982) "Five Stages of Growth in Small Businesses", *Long Range Planning*, 20:3, pp. 45-52

Sekaran, U. (1984) "The Research Process: Theoretical Framework, Hypothesis Development and Elements of Research Design"

Seringhaus, R. (1991) *Export Development and Promotion: The Role of Public Organizations*, Boston: Kluwer, Publishing

Sexton, D.L. & Van Auken, P. (1984) "A Longitudinal Study of Small Business Planning", *Journal of Small Business Management*, 22:2, pp. 6-15

Shaver, K.G. & Scott, L.R. (1991) "Person, Process and Choice: The Psychology of New Venture Creation", *Entrepreneurship Theory and Practice*, 16:2, pp. 23-46

Simon, H. (1957) *Administrative Behavior*, Second Edition, New York: Macmillan Company

Simpson, C. Jr. & Kujawa, D. (1974) "The Export Decision Process: An Empirical Inquiry", *Journal of International Business Studies*, 5:1, pp. 107-117

Singer, T.O. & Czinkota, M.R. (1992) "Factors Associated with the Effective Use of Export Assistance", working paper, pp. 1-30

Slevin, D. & Covin, J. (1989) "Strategic Management of Small Firms in Hostile and Benign Environments", *Strategic Management Journal*, 10:1, pp. 75-87

Slevin, D. & Covin, J. (1990) "New Venture Strategic Posture, Structure and Performance: An Industry Life Cycle Analysis", *Journal of Business Venturing*, 5:2, pp. 123-135

Slevin, D. & Covin, J. (1987) "The Competitive Tactics of Entrepreneurial Firms in High- and Low-Technology Industries", in Churchill, N.C., Hornaday, J.A., Kirchoff, B.A., Krasner, O.J., & Vesper, K.H. (eds.) *Frontiers of Entrepreneurship Research,* Proceedings of the Babson College Conference on Entrepreneurship, Wellesley, MA: Babson College, pp. 87-101

Slevin, D. & Covin, J., Covin, T. (1991) "Content and Performance of Growth Seeking Strategies: A Comparison of Small Firms in High- and Low-Technology Industries", *Journal of Business Venturing*, 5:6, pp. 391-412

Small Business in the American Economy, (1988), U.S. Government Printing Office, Washington, D.C.

Snaveley, W.P., Weiner, P., Ulbrich, H.H., & Enright, E.J.(1964) "Export Survey of the Greater Hartford Area", Vols. 1 & 2, in Miesenbock, K. (1988) "Small Business Exporting: A Literature Review", *International Small Business Journal*, Jan.-Mar., pp. 42-59

Spitzer, D., Alpar, P. & Hills, G. (1989) "Business Planning in New High Tech Firms", in Brockhaus, R.H., Churchill, N.C., Katz, J.A., Kirchoff, B.A., Vesper, K.H. & Wetzel, W.E., (eds.) *Frontiers of Entrepreneurship Research,* Proceedings of the Babson Conference on Entrepreneurship Research, pp. 389-407

Sriram, V. & Sapienza, H. (1991) "An Empirical Investigation of the Role of Marketing for Small Exporters", *Journal of Small Business Management*, 29:4, pp. 33-43

Starr, J.A. & MacMillan, I.C. (1990) "Resource Cooptation via Social Contracting: Resource Acquisition Strategies for New Ventures", *Strategic Management Journal*, 11: pp. 79-92

Stewart, A. (1991) "A Prospectus on the Anthropology of Entrepreneurship", *Entrepreneurship Theory and Practice*, 16:2, pp. 71-92

Stewart, R. (1992) "The Relationships and Relevance of New Venture Performance Measures"; Working Paper Northeastern University

Stevens, G.V.G. (1979) "The Determinants of Investment", in Dunning, J.H. (ed.) *Economic Analysis and the Multinational Enterprise*, New York: Praeger Publishing, pp.47-88

Stevens, J. (1986) *Applied Multivariate Statistics for the Social Sciences*, Hillsdale, NJ: Lawrence Erlbaum Assoc.

Stevenson, H.H. & Gumpert, D.E. (1985), "The Heart of Entrepreneurship", *Harvard Business Review,* Mar-Apr. pp. 85-94

Stinchcombe, A.L. (1965), "Social Structures and Organizations", in March, J.G. (ed.), *Handbook of Organizations*, Chicago: Rand McNally, pp. 142-193

Stone, M.S. & Brush, C.G. (1994) "Planning in Ambiguous Contexts: An Elaboration and Application of the Interpretive Model", under second revision for *Strategic Management Journal*

Stuart, R. & Abetti, P.A. (1987) "Start-Up Ventures: Towards the Prediction of Initial Success", *Journal of Business Venturing*, 2:3, pp. 215-230

Sullivan, D. & Bauerschmidt, A. (1990) "Incremental Internationalization: A Test of Johanson and Vahlne's Thesis", *Management International Review*, 30:1 pp. 19-30

Sullivan, D. & Bauerschmidt, A. (1991), "The 'Basic Concepts' of International Business Strategy: A Review and Reconsideration", *Management International Review*, Special Issue, pp. 111-124

Sullivan, R. (1994) "Getting Help to Fight Back", *Nation's Business*, Feb. p. 42

Suzman, C.L. & Wortzel, L.H. (1984) "Technology Profiles and Export Market Strategies", *Journal of Business Research*, Vol. 12, pp. 183-194

Tannenbaum (1991) *Wall Street Journal*, Nov. 30, 1991, p. B-2

Teece, D. (1983) "Technological and Organizational Factors in the Theory of the MNE" in Casson, M. (ed.) *The Growth of International Business,* London: Allen & Unwin

Telesio, P. (1979) *Technology Licensing and Multi-national Enterprises*, New York: Praeger Press

Tesar, G. (1977) "Identification of Planning, Attitudinal and Operational Differences Among Types of Exporters", *American Journal of Small Business,* 11:2, pp. 16-21

Timmons, J. (1985) *New Venture Creation,* 2nd Edition, Homewood, ILL: Richard D. Irwin

The State of Small Business, (1987), A Report of the President, Washington, D.C.: U.S. Government Printing Office

The State of Small Business, (1989), A Report of the President, Washington, D.C.: U.S. Government Printing Office

The State of Small Business, (1990), A Report of the President, Washington, D.C.: U.S. Government Printing Office

Thorelli, H. (1987) "Entrepreneurship in International Marketing: Some Research Opportunities", in Hills, G.E., (ed.) *Research at the Marketing/Entrepreneurship Interface*, University of Chicago at Illinois, published by United States Association for Small Business and Entrepreneurship, pp. 183-204

Tookey, D.A. (1964) "Factors Associated with Success in Exporting", *The Journal of Management Studies,* 1:1, pp. 48-66

Toyne, B. (1989) "International Exchange: A Foundation for Theory Building in International Business", *Journal of International Business Studies*, 20:1, pp. 1-17

Tyebjee, T. (1990) "The Internationalization of High Tech Ventures" in Churchill, N.C., Bygrave, W.B., Hornaday, J.A., Muzyka, D., Vesper, K.H. & Wetzel, W.E. Jr. (eds.) *Frontiers of Entrepreneurship Research*, Proceedings of the Babson Conference on Entrepreneurship Research, pp. 452-467

Ursic, M.L. & Czinkota, M.R. (1984) "An Experience Curve Explanation for Export Expansion", *Journal of Business Research*, 112:2, pp. 159-168

U.S. Import/Export Directory, (1989), Washington, D.C.: Department of Commerce, Office of Trade and Development

Vachani, S. (1991) "A Longitudinal Study of the Bargaining Power of American, British and Other European Multinationals in India Between 1973-1987", Working Paper, Boston University

Vachani, S. (1990) "Distinguishing Between Related and Unrelated International Geographic Diversification: A Comprehensive Measure of Global Diversification", *Journal of International Business Studies*, 21:2, pp. 307-322

VanderWerf, P.A. & Brush, C.G. (1989) "Achieving Empirical Progress in an Undefined Field", *Entrepreneurship Theory & Practice,* 14:2, pp. 45-58

Van de Ven, A.H., Hudson, R. & Schroeder, D.M. (1984) "Designing New Business Start-ups: Entrepreneurial, Organizational and Ecological Considerations", *Journal of Management*, 10:1 pp. 87-107

Vernon, R. (1966) "International Investment and International Trade in the Product Cycle", *Quarterly Journal of Economics*, 80: pp. 190-207

Vernon, R. (1974) "The Location of Industry", in Dunning, J.H. (ed.) *Economic Analysis and the Multinational Enterprise*, London, George Allen & Unwin

Vesper, K. (1990) *New Venture Strategies*, 2nd Ed., Englewood Cliffs, NJ: Prentice Hall

Wall Street Journal (1990), "Enterprise", Nov. 8, p. A-2

Wall Street Journal (1990), "Three Small Businesses Profit by Taking on the World", Oct. 13, p. A-2

Walters, G.P. & Samiee, S. (1990) "A Model for Assessing Performance in Small U.S. Exporting Firms", *Entrepreneurship Theory and Practice*, 15:2, pp. 33-50

Walters, G.P. (1993) "Patterns of Formal Planning and Performance in U.S. Exporting Firms", *Management International Review*, 33:1, pp. 43-63

Weick, K (1984) *The Social Psychology of Organizing*, 2nd Edition, New York: Random House

Weidersheim-Paul, F., Olson, C. H. & Welch, L. (1978) "Pre-Export Activity: The First Step in Internationalization", *Journal of International Business Studies*, 9:1, pp. 47-58

Welch, L S. & Wiedersheim-Paul, F. (1980) "Initial Exports- A Marketing Failure?" *The Journal of Management Studies,* 17:4, pp. 334-344

Welch, L.S. & Loustarinen, R. (1988) "Internationalization: Evolution of a Concept", *Journal of General Management,* 14:2, pp. 34-55

Williamson, O.E. (1978) *Markets and Hierarchies: Analysis and Antitrust Implications*, New York: The Free Press

Withey, J.J. (1980) "Differences Between Exporters and Non-Exporters: Some Hypotheses Concerning Small Manufacturing Businesses", *American Journal of Small Business*, 4:3 pp. 29-37

Yaprak, A. (1985) "An Empirical Study of the Differences Between Small Exporting and Non-exporting U.S. Firms", *International Marketing Review*, 2:2, pp. 72-83

Zeller, R.A. & Carmines, E.G. (1980), *Measurement in the Social Sciences: The Link Between Theory and Data*, London: Cambridge University Press

Index

For Product Safety Concerns and Information please contact our EU
representative GPSR@taylorandfrancis.com Taylor & Francis Verlag GmbH,
Kaufingerstraße 24, 80331 München, Germany

Printed and bound by CPI Group (UK) Ltd, Croydon, CR0 4YY
05/05/2025
01860818-0001